CHRISTIANS AND ALCOHOL

This is the second of a series of booklets being published for the Church of England National Council for Social Aid. They are primarily intended to help Christians think more clearly about the moral and theological implications of some of the major problems facing society today. It is hoped, however, that the series will be of interest to non-Christians, as well as being seen as a contribution towards a wider public discussion.

The first booklet in this series was *Christians and Gambling*. Further titles will include:

Christians and Delinquents
Christians and Drugs
Christians and AIDS

* * * *

The Church of England National Council for Social Aid was formed in 1969 to take over the work of the Church of England Temperance Society and the National Police Court Mission. These organisations were initially responsible for the establishment of the Probation and After Care Service in England and Wales, stemming from the services provided for the courts to deal with alcoholic offenders and those within prisons.

The Council, which is an independent charity, is currently engaged in promoting better community services for offenders and those addicted to drink, drugs or gambling. It has been a pioneer in the provision of services and facilities for those with special needs in the community, and is concerned to identify gaps within the welfare system and to establish agencies to meet them in co-operation with both statutory and voluntary bodies working in similar and related fields.

General Secretary
National Council for Social Aid
38 Ebury Street, London SW1W 0LU

CHRISTIANS AND ALCOHOL

A Christian Response to Alcohol Misuse in Society

National Council for Social Aid

ISBN 0 951 35601 1

First published 1989 by the Church of England National Council for Social Aid

Phototypeset and printed by
Richard Clay Ltd, Bungay, Suffolk

FOREWORD

In the mid-nineteenth century, a number of clergymen in the Church of England were troubled by the scale of alcohol misuse in their society. Most confined their concern to the problems which confronted them in their own parish until Mrs Wightman, the wife of the Vicar of St Alkmond, published a book *Haste to the Rescue* in 1859. A copy was sent to every clergyman in the country and many were inspired to establish a church temperance society in their parish. The outcome of this movement was the founding of the Church of England Temperance Society and *Haste to the Rescue* became its cornerstone.

Some 130 years on, we find that the consumption of alcohol and the harm which it causes continues to constitute a major problem in our society. Yet such is the pervasiveness and social acceptability of alcohol that any attempt to prohibit its use would be futile even if it were thought to be desirable. It is therefore essential that preventive action is taken to control its widespread misuse in the community.

Local churches, at the heart of their communities, have a crucial role to play in promoting socially responsible attitudes towards the consumption of alcohol. They can also offer understanding, compassion and support to those experiencing problems with their drinking. In order to be effective, Christians need to know the facts about alcohol and its effects and how they can help problem drinkers.

Christians and Alcohol is based on our experience in developing alcohol awareness programmes for clergy and other church groups in a number of dioceses. We hope that the information in this booklet will be of interest to Christians in the Anglican community as well as other denominations.

Easter 1989

The Rt Revd Colin Docker
Chairman of the Council

ACKNOWLEDGEMENTS

We are deeply indebted to Mr Tom Ross, former director of the North Yorkshire Council on Alcoholism, for his help in preparing this booklet and to our General Secretary, the Revd E. W. F. Agar, for editing the material. We are also most grateful to the following for their valuable comments on the booklet, although they are in no way responsible for any of its shortcomings: the Revd Dr Christopher Cunliffe, Fellow and Chaplain of Lincoln College, University of Oxford; Dr Vivien Deacon, Consultant Psychiatrist, Norman House Day Hospital, Harrogate; Mr Peter Carlin, Director, Buckinghamshire Council on Alcohol and Drugs.

Our thanks are also due to the following organisations for their help with reference material: Alcohol Concern, Action on Alcohol Abuse, and the York Alcohol Advice Service.

We have quoted extensively from a number of publications. All are acknowledged throughout the text and we are grateful to each publisher for permission to reproduce their material.

CONTENTS

INTRODUCTION

Alcohol misuse has been described as 'the major public health issue of our time, overshadowing even that of tobacco and dwarfing the problems of illicit drug abuse'. So begins a report published by the Royal College of Psychiatrists in 1986.[1] The Psychiatrists' observations were backed up by similar reports from the Royal College of Physicians and the Royal College of General Practitioners.[2] There is therefore wide recognition by medical specialists that the abuse of alcohol represents a significant threat to the nation's health. The World Health Organisation has a similar concern and acknowledges alcohol as the third greatest cause of premature death after heart disease and cancer.[3]

Apart from the personal health risks, we are learning to recognise alcohol as a significant factor in social and family problems. Alarm is currently being expressed in response to hooliganism and street violence which is associated with heavy drinking. The whole nation has experienced a sense of disgrace regarding the behaviour of a small minority of football fans who have become our least popular export to our European neighbours. The links between alcohol and other forms of crime have been well documented and many inmates in our overcrowded prisons may have a drinking problem.

The government faces a number of dilemmas in managing the nation's drinking problems. While, on the one hand, they favour a relaxation of some liquor licensing legislation, there is an acknowledged need to restrain the excesses of young heavy drinkers and to enforce rigorously drink-driving legislation. There are also internal and external pressures on the government to reduce further the cost of alcoholic drinks with an associated risk that overall consumption, which has plateaued in recent years, could escalate once again. The Church is inevitably drawn into public debate over some of these issues as the decisions which will be taken could have far-reaching effects on the social fabric of the nation.

While some Christians may wrestle with these national issues, all are faced with the challenge of alcohol misuse as it confronts us in our local communities. It is clear that a traditional conception of 'alcoholism' as a disease, to which a small minority of the population are genetically disposed, would not equip us to respond to the various manifestations of alcohol misuse which are now acknowledged. Professional perspectives on alcohol problems and, consequently, forms of service provision, have been changing radically in the last twenty years. A move away from centralisation and specialisation of alcohol services has led to more community-orientated services in which greater value is placed on informal helpers and volunteer counsellors.

The National Council for Social Aid (NCSA) has recognised that, for the Church to be fully responsive to alcohol misuse today, Christians need to be in touch with current trends and, more importantly, working together with local and national agencies in tackling our society's alcohol problems. In 1983, the NCSA began a programme of action which is now culminating in the publication of this book. First of all, a memorandum was produced – 'The Way Ahead' – which was partly a response to the 1982 DHSS Report 'Drinking Sensibly'. In it, the NCSA stated its position on the use and misuse of alcohol:

> The NCSA is not opposed to the sensible use of alcohol, but it is concerned with the harmful effects arising from its misuse . . . alcohol abuse is a growing problem in society . . . in order to reduce its impact there must be effective preventive measures as well as a comprehensive range of services and facilities for those with serious drinking problems and for their families.

The memorandum contained recommendations for courses of action which would help alleviate alcohol-related problems. These included a call for more resources to be put into health education on alcohol so that 'every person in whose life alcohol plays a part can make responsible decisions based on facts'. Not only did the NCSA seek action from the Government, it also embarked on its own alcohol awareness programme.

This programme developed out of an understanding that,

within the Church, there was a lack of information about alcohol problems and how to handle them. Moreover, it was known that counsellors, working with problem drinkers, find that there are problems peculiar to families where there is more than a nominal adherence to a Christian way of life. For example, individuals from Christian backgrounds may experience a greater burden of guilt associated with excessive drinking. It seemed important, therefore, that the clergy be made more fully aware of the true nature and extent of alcohol problems.

The practical outworking of this conviction took the form of a series of seminars which were organised on a diocesan basis. The first three study programmes were carefully monitored and became the basis for a research study.[4] Organisation of each diocesan event was the responsibility of a local planning group which included representatives of the NCSA and the respective Boards of Social Responsibility alongside local alcohol specialists from voluntary and statutory services. Each programme had the same basic objectives:

(i) To give clergy and other groups some basic information about alcohol and its effects.
(ii) To explain how clergy and others can be more involved with alcohol problems.
(iii) To make clergy more aware of local resources.

The first pilot study took place in the Diocese of Chichester in 1984 and, following on from its initial success, the programme was extended to the Dioceses of Canterbury and Rochester in 1985, Ripon in 1986, and Liverpool in 1988. The one-day seminars were made open to all members of the clergy, accredited lay ministers and other church groups, including representatives from other denominations. *Christians and Alcohol*, therefore, is a development of these diocesan programmes and will hopefully serve to communicate the facts and the issues to a wider audience. It is aimed primarily at clergy and concerned laity in British churches but should also be of value to alcohol specialists who need to understand Christian perspectives on alcohol misuse. The intention is to provide a handbook rather than a workshop manual. Consequently, it does not provide a full discussion of the cultural, social and environmental factors which affect drinking behaviour, or international differences in patterns of alcohol use. Readers who wish to follow up these aspects should consult Appendix B at the end of the book.

Those who believe that theology is best served by amassing texts from the Bible will be disappointed. In our view, this would be a fruitless exercise. Instead, we have tried to provide some guidelines for a Christian understanding of and response to the use and misuse of alcohol. We have done no more than take a few exploratory steps in a field which is ripe for further theological study. Those Christians who wish to work with problem drinkers will find some useful pointers in Chapter 4 but, if they wish to develop counselling skills, they are advised to consult the recommended books in Appendix B.

Above all, *Christians and Alcohol* is aimed at those who have an active concern for the problems of alcohol misuse and are charged with the responsibility to care constructively for individuals and families where alcohol has become a problem. We trust that the contents are not only informative but are also challenging. The statistics presented may prick our consciences but it is an understanding of the personal human tragedies behind the figures which must move our hearts.

1

FACTS ABOUT ALCOHOL

The history of every civilisation includes references to alcohol and, even though some cultures have prohibited it, its use is now worldwide. The production of alcoholic drinks has been affected by many refinements through the ages and is now one of the major industries in the western world.

In this first chapter, we will look at some basic facts that Christians ought to know about alcohol and consider the many ways in which it is used in our society. We will also attempt to draw some distinction between use and misuse.

Our Favourite Drug

A recent report by the Royal College of Psychiatrists was titled 'Alcohol, Our Favourite Drug'.[1] Published at a time when media attention was focusing on the nation's escalating drug problems involving heroin and cocaine, the report stressed that alcohol constituted a far greater risk to health and well-being. Thus, the first and most important fact to acknowledge is that alcohol is an extremely potent and dangerous drug.

It may be unlike most other drugs in that it is readily available without prescription, it is relatively easy to manufacture, and it has innumerable diverse applications; yet it is unquestionably a mood-altering substance. Stripped of its aeons of social use and acceptability and presented as a new discovery, it would undoubtedly be classified as a dangerous drug and be subject to all appropriate statutory controls. As it is, too many people use alcohol without any accurate knowledge of its nature and effects. Errors in perception of alcohol are common. Some of the following basic facts about alcohol are the exact opposite of what many drinkers believe.

(i) Alcohol is a depressant. It is common to use alcohol as a stimulant but the opposite is true. Its apparent initial stimulant effects result from the loss of inhibitions. If drinking is sustained, other mental and physical faculties are diminished as the drug progressively affects the nervous system. Loss of balance, dulled hearing, blurred vision, slurred speech, and even loss of bladder control can be experienced if too much alcohol is consumed in one session. Someone who is 'under the influence' is out of touch with reality and is, to some extent, 'out of control'. An intoxicated person may feel alert and confident and may even feel that he or she is a better driver. The reality is completely different.

(ii) Alcohol is a poison. Chemists handle many different alcohols, most of which are highly toxic and are labelled accordingly. Ethyl alcohol, with the chemical formula C_2H_5OH, is exceptional in that, in solution with water, it is considered fit for human consumption. Nevertheless, a small but significant number of people die in this country each year simply because they drink too much in one session and lapse into unconsciousness with fatal consequences. Regular drinkers build up a tolerance to alcohol which diminishes this particular risk.

However, too much alcohol over a long period of time can damage most organs of the body. In addition to liver disease, there are a long list of medical complaints attributable to alcohol use, including hypertension, gastric ulcers, pancreatitis, peripheral neuritis, heart disease, and cancers of the larynx and pharynx. Brain damage is one of the most disturbing consequences of heavy drinking and is manifest in subtle reductions in mental functioning as well as in severe dementia (see Table 1).

TABLE 1

Physical and Psychological Consequences of Heavy Drinking

GENERAL HEALTH	Increased susceptibility to various forms of infection. Poor nutrition leading to obesity and/or vitamin deficiency. Low levels of self-awareness; therefore first symptoms of major disorders may be missed by heavy drinker.
MENTAL HEALTH	Depression, anxiety, and various forms of neurosis are likely. Heavy drinker may be moody, fluctuating from deep depression to aggressive outbursts. Alcohol may be used to relieve symptoms of mental illness, delaying more appropriate care.
BRAIN and NERVOUS SYSTEM	Intellectual functioning is impaired: poor problem solving and decision making. Short-term memory may be affected (blackouts) and, in severe cases, brain damage may occur (Korsakoff's psychosis or Wernicke's encephalopathy). Withdrawal from intoxication may involve shakiness and, in severe cases, fits and delirium tremens (DTs) are possible. Peripheral neuritis, loss of sensation at the extremities, is a long-term effect of heavy drinking.
REPRODUCTIVE SYSTEM	Loss of libido in both male and female heavy drinkers is common. In men, production of semen may be affected with an associated low sperm count. In women, the menstrual cycle may be disrupted and the vagina can become dry, leading to problems during intercourse. Drinking during pregnancy may increase the risk of miscarriage and can affect the fetus.
DIGESTIVE SYSTEM	Before it reaches the stomach, alcohol can cause damage and may increase the risk of cancer in the mouth, throat, and oesophagus. Inflammation of the stomach lining (acute gastritis) is common and ulcers can be aggravated. The pancreas is affected and acute pancreatitis is particularly common in young male drinkers.
CARDIOVASCULAR SYSTEM	Alcohol affects the heart muscle and may cause chronic heart disease. Strokes may be brought on by heavy drinking. High blood pressure is possible and the blood's clotting ability is reduced by alcohol. The suggestion that moderate alcohol use helps prevent coronary disease is open to question.
LIVER	Fatty liver, alcoholic hepatitis, liver cancer and cirrhosis may develop. Symptoms of these conditions may take many years to appear. In most cases, liver damage will only be arrested with abstinence.

(iii) All beers reach the same parts. There are a wide range of different alcoholic drinks with many colours, tastes and textures. However, their intoxicating effects are determined solely by the percentage of alcohol in each drink. It is helpful to think in terms of 'Standard Units' of alcohol. That is, $\frac{1}{2}$ pint of beer or cider = 1 glass of wine = 1 single measure of spirits = 1 measure of fortified wine = 1 Standard Unit. Hence, the alcoholic effect of drinking fifteen pints of normal beer is about the same as drinking one bottle of whisky. Other substances in drinks, called congeners, can have physical side-effects (e.g. influence the likelihood of hangovers) but they cannot increase the potency of the alcohol. Figure 1 displays the relative strengths for different types of alcoholic drink.

FIGURE 1

What is a unit of alcohol?

As soon as alcohol is received into the stomach and intestines, it begins to be absorbed into the bloodstream which carries it to every part of the body. Only about 2 to 5 per cent of alcohol consumed can pass out of the body unchanged via the kidneys, lungs and sweat glands. The remainder must be processed by the liver at the rate of approximately 1 standard unit per hour. While this process cannot be accelerated, the rate of absorption can be affected by different factors.

The higher the concentration of alcohol in the original drink, the quicker the alcohol will pass into the bloodstream. If the drink is fizzy it will be absorbed quickly but, if it is sweet, it is absorbed slowly. Eating also slows down the rate of absorption. The quicker alcohol is absorbed, the higher will be the concentration in the bloodstream and likewise the immediate intoxication effects.

However, the total length of time during which there is alcohol in the bloodstream is unchanged. It is like a bucket with a slow leak. You can fill it slowly or quickly but it will take the same time to empty. Consequently, 'sleeping it off' is not sufficient for some drivers who can still produce a positive breath test the morning after the night before.

(iv) Alcohol affects women differently. Men and women have different proportions of body fat and water. Women, with more fat and less water, can drink the same amount of alcohol as a man but experience a higher concentration of alcohol in the bloodstream. Therefore, three pints of beer can put a man over the legal limit for driving while only two pints would produce the same result in a woman. This applies even when different body weights are taken into account.

Pregnant women have to be particularly careful with alcohol and are normally advised to abstain completely for the duration of the pregnancy. There is some evidence that even moderate amounts of alcohol in the early stages of pregnancy can increase the risk of miscarriage. Excessive consumption of alcohol can damage the fetus at any stage. The extreme consequence of this is a condition known as 'fetal alcohol syndrome'. A child born with this has distinct facial features and is likely to be mentally retarded.

(v) Alcohol has long-term effects. Some of the physical effects of long-term heavy drinking have been outlined above. Mental and personality effects, although less clearly understood, are also very evident. Certainly, intellectual ability can be impaired and this is measurable. Personality changes, the consequence of long-term exposure to a depressant drug, are more subtle and have knock-on effects in interpersonal relationships. A negative outlook on life is observable in many problem drinkers. This mitigates against sustained recovery and contributes to the vicious circles of dependence which will be considered more fully in a later chapter.

Sensible Drinking?

Given that there are so many potential negative effects of alcohol, is it reasonable to discuss the notion of safe drinking levels? It must be recognised, as we have mentioned at the beginning of this chapter, that alcohol is a dangerous drug and those who choose consciously to use it must be aware of the attendant risks. Figure 2 is a simple graph which plots 'chance of having alcohol-related problem', whether physical, mental or social, against 'average daily level of consumption'.

FIGURE 2

The Risk Curve

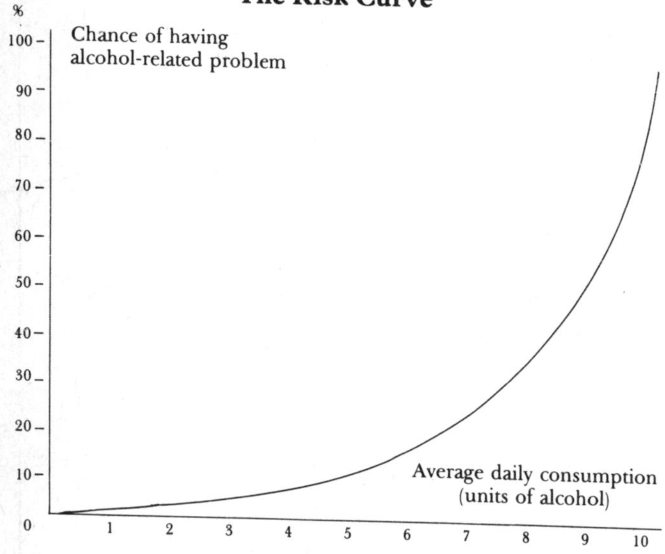

The message is simple. The more you drink, the more likely you are to have problems. Someone who drinks, on average, the equivalent of half a pint of beer per day, is most unlikely to have a problem. An exception would be the man who goes out once a month and drinks fifteen pints in one session. On the other hand, someone regularly consum-

FIGURE 3

Weekly Drinking Targets

	Women Units	Men Units
Aim at this level for least risk	up to 14	up to 21
Watch your drinking	15–21	22–35
Cut down now	over 21	over 35

(1 unit = ½ pint beer/1 glass wine/1 tot spirits)
Source: The Drinking Revolution (1987), Alcohol Concern.

ing over four pints of beer per day is almost certain to experience some harm associated with their drinking. Research suggests that about 3.5 per cent of Britian's adult population (i.e. almost two million) fall into this category.[2] Most experts (e.g. Health Education Authority, Royal College of Psychiatrists, Alcohol Concern) currently advocate a weekly upper limit of twenty-one units for men and fourteen units for women. This quantity should, of course, be spread over the week. Two or three pints, two or three times a week (or the woman's equivalent) is good advice but less is even better.

However, the quantity of alcohol consumed is not the sole factor in determining risk. One might drink moderately for years and then, in response to a bereavement, begin to take consolation from alcohol. Another might drink moderately except for a one-off celebration and stupidly drive off to his death in a road traffic accident. Previous consumption alone could not predict these eventualities.

It is conceivable that the sensible drinking levels advocated today may, in the light of a few more years' experience, be lowered further. Nevertheless, it is helpful to view the agreed upper limits as benchmarks against which responsible drinkers can compare their pattern of consumption. Figure 3 provides a useful illustration of weekly drinking targets for men and women.

For those who are prepared to take risks with their drinking, there is a challenge to 'Cut down now' if they are exceeding twenty-one units (women) and thirty-five units (men) per week. For Christians, the message is clear: moderation in all things.

Under the Influence

The presence of alcohol follows us from the cradle to the grave. From the moment when the first teaspoon of gripe water (containing alcohol) is administered, we are, whether we like it or not, subject, by some degree or another, to the subtle or overt influence of alcohol. 'Wetting the baby's head' is just one amongst hundreds of social rituals whose efficacy appears to depend on the consumption of alcoholic drinks. Christenings, birthdays, Christmases, engagements, weddings, and even funerals are all family occasions which rarely pass without the presence of alcohol. The toasting of success, a modern equivalent for the dispensation of blessing, involves an almost sacred allegiance to alcohol. The social pressure, often expressed verbally, is that 'it wouldn't be the same without IT'.

Everyone, in a sense, tends to be an 'occasional' drinker because every 'occasion' provides an excuse to drink. Winning a motor race or a cup final and launching a ship are events which are traditionally accompanied by showers of champagne. What applies to public life influences individual experiences of life events. Personal successes are often accompanied by heavy drinking sessions. Curiously, personal disasters can also lead to 'drowning one's sorrows'. Indeed, alcohol is used both as a social lubricant and as a popular panacea. There is no need to list all the uses of alcohol here. Take five minutes, a blank sheet of paper and a small group of people. See how many different reasons for drinking you can think of and write them down. You will soon run out of space and you will find the exercise to be very revealing.

For many people in our society, drinking is not occasional. It is a daily practice. The local pub or club is the centre of their social life and their alcohol consumption, although increased from time to time in response to various life events, is steady and habitual. Consequently, with respect to general consumer expenditure, spending on alcohol comes third after housing and food. People spend more on alcohol than they do on clothes or on transport or on home decoration. The reality is, therefore, that British people, having met the most basic of human needs—shelter and nourishment—put alcohol as their next priority. This commitment to alcohol costs us £45 million each day, over £500 per second.[3]

Some readers may recoil from this picture of a nation whose social infrastructure is so dominated by the use of a potent drug. However, we should be careful not to give way to fear and adopt a rigid anti-drinking position. Those who do choose an alcohol-free lifestyle should do so out of personal conviction rather than as a reaction to society's excesses. Most Christians who do drink have a responsible attitude to alcohol which is underpinned by basic beliefs concerning personal conduct and social responsibility. They enjoy drinking in moderation and their drinking practices provide a good example for their children and a good model for society.

However, society's norms are not necessarily Christian norms and we must guard ourselves and our children against pressures which push us into risky drinking practices. It is inevitable then that each one of us will face many difficult decisions concerning alcohol in the course of our lives. Established social practices, coupled with the persuasive messages of the brewers and distillers, combine to push individuals into a potentially harmful conformity. As we will see in the next chapter, following the crowd is not without its costs.

2

HOW BIG IS THE PROBLEM?

No set of statistics can adequately sum up the innumerable personal tragedies that are consequential to alcohol misuse. However, this chapter will serve its purpose if, in response to data which reveals the prevalence of the problem, Christians are more ready to identify and respond appropriately to the incidences on their own doorsteps.

We can begin by painting the picture of alcohol misuse in the nation with a very broad brush. Roughly speaking, alcohol problems are generated by three types of drinking behaviour.

(a) *Regular Use*

A recent paper by Professor R. E. Kendell included this very significant observation on alcohol-related harm—'because moderate drinkers are so much more numerous than heavy drinkers, the greater part of the ill-effects experienced by the community as a whole are generated by comparatively moderate drinkers'.[1] Most people think of 'problem drinking' in terms of public drunkenness and an outdated concept of 'alcoholism'. Professor Kendell's point is that most alcohol-related harm is the result of drinking practices which are generally acceptable in our society. The regular intake of alcohol in excessive amounts over a period of time takes its toll on the human body irrespective of whether the drinker ever gets drunk or becomes dependent.

(b) *Intoxication*

This is the most public aspect of problem drinking. The link between intoxication and public disorder, domestic violence, road casualties and all sorts of accidental injury is well documented. Few people, however, appreciate the full scale of the harm which is caused directly by drunkenness.

(c) *Dependence*

'Alcoholism', in its traditional sense, is only the tip of the iceberg. Even so, its imagery is very powerful and still dominates many people's perception of all alcohol-related problems. Certainly, the personal suffering associated with addiction is particularly acute and continues to demand a lot of attention.

To complement the above outline, it is helpful to identify three areas of consequence. Each problem area has either legal, medical or social consequences for society, or a mixture of those. For example, the consequences of intoxication are mainly legal (i.e. demanding the attention of the police and the courts), whereas the consequences of 'regular use' are mainly medical (i.e. demanding Health Service resources). On the other hand, the consequences of 'dependence' are mainly social (i.e. family breakdown).

These can be linked in a simple diagram (see Figure 4). It may be helpful to keep this grid in mind as we go on to examine some specific problem areas.

Health

The greatest burden of care for the victims of alcohol misuse falls on the National Health Service. Road accidents and the scenes in casualty departments on Friday and Saturday evenings make the headlines, but hospitals also have to treat a whole range of physical problems which are the direct result of years of excessive drinking. One of the most startling health statistics reveals that one in four of emergency and general medical admissions can be attributed directly or indirectly to alcohol consumption.[2] One of the most reliable indicators of the nation's health is the number of deaths from chronic liver disease and cirrhosis. The rate of these deaths per 100,000 total population rose from 2.8 in 1970 to 4.6 in 1984.[3] The NHS psychiatric services are also fully occupied in response to alcohol problems. About 17,000 out of 180,000 admissions to psychiatric hospitals

FIGURE 4

Consequences of Alcohol Misuse

	Legal	Medical	Social
REGULAR DRINKING	Marginal but risk of driving offence is increased.	Substantial long-term physical damage is major drain on medical services.	Ill-health puts some pressure on family life and relationships.
INTOXICATION	Drunkenness in itself (or when driving) is an offence and alcohol is a major factor in many forms of crime.	Accidents and trauma have severe medical consequences, causing many sudden deaths.	Major factor in family violence. Even one incident can damage relationships.
DEPENDENCE	Habitual drunken offenders represent a major dilemma to legal system. Factor in divorce actions.	Psychiatric services have major interest in treating dependence.	Loss of job and marriage breakdown is common. Risk of social alienation.

each year are connected with alcohol abuse.[4] Moreover, 66 per cent of suicide attempts and deaths involve alcohol.[5]

Accidents

Sudden deaths caused by accidents of any kind are particularly tragic. For many grieving relatives, the trauma is exacerbated by the knowledge that alcohol was the major cause of the accident. The death toll makes grim reading.

— As many as 27 per cent of persons killed on the roads of England and Wales in one year (1,400 fatalities) have had blood alcohol levels over the legal limit.[6]

— Alcohol has been shown to be a factor in:
    19 per cent of all drownings,[7]
    39 per cent of fire deaths,[8]
    43 per cent of deaths from falls,[9]

and 30 per cent of all accidental deaths in the 51 to 64 age group.[10]

In considering road accidents it is worth noting that the legal limit is not a safe limit. Research indicates that the risk of having an accident is doubled when the legal limit of 80 mg per cent alcohol is reached.

Crime

The presence of alcohol is an undisputed factor in a wide range of criminal offences, most of which are not premeditated. Public disorder related to alcohol abuse, for example football hooliganism, has been identified as a particular problem in Britain.

— Offences of drunkenness in England and Wales rose from 68,109 in 1960 to a 'staggering' 122,259 in 1980.[11] Partly to relieve the burden on the courts and the penal system, new cautioning procedures were introduced in the 'eighties. On paper, there has therefore been a significant reduction in convictions since then.
— In 1968, after the current 'breathalyser' law was introduced, there were 18,374 convictions for drunken driving in England and Wales. In 1984, there were 101,000.[12]
— In 1983, about 45 per cent of offences of wounding and assault were committed by people thought by their victims to be drinking.[13] Drinking is a factor in 50 per cent of homicides.[14]

Employment

Between eight and fourteen million working days are lost each year due to heavy drinking.[15] There is no record of the cost to industry related to the impaired judgement of key decision-makers. However, there is an association between occupation and the likelihood of developing alcohol-related disabilities (see Table 2).

Young People

Young people, if physically mature, can drink heavily

without necessarily being conscious of the immediate negative physical effects. However, their emotional development is likely to suffer and they may be laying the seeds of medical and other associated problems which will develop in later life. Many young heavy drinkers, however, do not survive that long. Alcohol is reckoned to be the biggest single cause of premature death in young men in this country.

— Drink is a factor in 45 per cent of fatal road accidents to young people.[16] One-third of all drink-driving offences are committed by under-25s.[17]
— 38 per cent of drownings in the 25–29 age group are alcohol related.[18]
— While the general trend in drunkenness convictions in

TABLE 2

Standardized mortality ratios of different occupations for cirrhosis of the liver, England and Wales, 1970–72

	Standardized mortality ratio
Average occupation	100
Publicans, innkeepers	1576
Deck, engineering officers and pilots, ships	781
Barmen, barmaids	633
Deck and engine-room ratings, barge and boatmen	628
Fishermen	595
Proprietors and managers, boarding houses and hotels	506
Finance, insurance brokers, financial agents	392
Restaurateurs	385
Lorry drivers' mates, van guards	377
Armed forces (British and foreign)	367
Cooks	354
Shunters, pointsmen	323
Winders, reelers	319
Electrical engineers	316
Authors, journalists, and related workers	314
Medical practitioners	311

Note: By definition the average standardized mortality ratio is 100, so barmen and barmaids, for example, have a cirrhosis mortality more than six times the average.
Source: Office of Population Censuses and Surveys, 1978.

recent years has been downward (see under Crime above), the proportion of under-21s has risen from 20 per cent in 1974 to 26 per cent in 1984.[19]

We will consider the underlying trends which give rise to heavy drinking amongst young people in the final chapter.

Women

While men drink much more than women and more men than women develop drink problems, the pattern has been changing in recent years. Evidence suggests that problems in women are increasing more rapidly than in men.

— Between 1975 and 1985, female convictions for drink-driving offences increased by 225 per cent compared to a 45 per cent rise for men.[20]
— Between 1973 and 1983, female convictions for drunkenness increased by 22 per cent compared to a 3 per cent rise for men.[21]
— Between 1979 and 1985, female deaths from chronic liver disease and cirrhosis increased by 18 per cent compared to a 12 per cent rise for men.[22]

Family Life

Campaigns against the 'evils of alcohol' have traditionally focused on its effects on family life. Wife battering and child abuse do accompany heavy drinking but the subtler effects of alcohol misuse can be equally devastating. It is likely that alcohol is a factor in one in three of divorce actions. Child abuse has hit the headlines in the 1980s but little mention is made of the fact that heavy drinking is a stress factor in 20.5 per cent of cases.[23]

Adding It All Up

An overall picture of the effects of alcohol misuse in any society involves estimating the mortality, the number of premature deaths, and the economic costs. The Addiction Research Centre at York University have been studying these figures for a number of years and their findings are worthy of our close attention.

The mortality associated with alcohol arises from a range

of accidents as well as from cirrhosis and other physical conditions. Using death certificates alone, the Addiction Research Centre calculated that there were between 5,000 and 7,800 alcohol-related deaths in 1982.[24] However, death certificates are not a reliable source as physicians may be reluctant to disclose the alcohol factor with regard to the sensitivities of relatives. Estimates of the full extent of alcohol-related mortality vary considerably but there are likely to be at least 25,000 deaths per annum.

The social and economic costs are equally difficult to

TABLE 3

The Resource Costs of Alcohol Misuse in England and Wales (1985 prices)

1. The Social Cost to Industry	£m
(a) Sickness absence	723.55
(b) Housework services	48.60
(c) Unemployment	166.74
(d) Premature deaths	653.31
2. Social Costs to the National Health Service	
(a) Psychiatric hospitals, inpatient costs (alcoholic psychosis, alcoholic dependence syndrome, non-dependent use of alcohol)	19.89
(b) Non-psychiatric hospitals, inpatient costs (alcohol psychosis, alcohol dependence syndrome alcoholic cirrhosis and liver disease)	8.04
(c) Other alcohol-related inpatient costs	82.09
(d) General practice costs	2.1
3. Society's Response to Alcohol-Related Problems	
(a) Expenditure by National alcohol bodies	0.33
(b) Research	0.60
4. Social Cost of Material Damage	
(a) Road traffic accidents (damage)	104.01
5. Social Costs of Criminal Activities	
(a) Police involvement in traffic offences (excluding road traffic accidents)	4.90
(b) Police involvement in road traffic offences (including judiciary and insurance administration)	14.53
(c) Drink related court cases	18.14
TOTAL (excluding unemployment and premature death)	1026.78
TOTAL (including unemployment and premature death)	1846.83

Source: Maynard, Hardman & Whelan (1987), *British Journal of Addiction*, Vol. 82.

evaluate accurately. Nevertheless, the findings outlined in Table 3 are widely accepted as a conservative estimate of the nation's bill for alcohol-related damage.

Adding inflation to these 1985 prices, we can estimate that, in 1989, the total cost of alcohol misuse will easily top £2.2 billion but may even be much higher.

Faced with this toll of human misery and economic waste, we cannot but conclude that alcohol misuse is Britain's single biggest social problem. Tobacco may be a factor in more physical sickness and premature death but smoking is not known to cause violence or break up families. Alcohol misuse then is a problem which our society must come to terms with and which the Church must vigorously address.

3

CHRISTIAN PERSPECTIVES

In the last chapter, we outlined the nature and extent of alcohol misuse in Britain today. While there is an urgent need to develop strategics for combating alcohol misuse in society, there is another side to the equation. As Christians, we are most effective when we are responding not only to the needs of men, but also to the commissioning of God.

It is not immediately apparent, however, that there is a single clearly defined Christian response to the phenomenon of alcohol misuse. The evidence of the biblical writings and of Christian teaching as it has developed throughout history reflects the complexity of the issues. And this is not surprising, for Christian ethical teaching does not—or should not—develop in a vacuum. It is a response to the challenges of facing the society of which the Church is part.

Issues of principle do, however, press their claims in this debate, as in others. In trying to come to a common mind on many ethical issues Christians have to reconcile apparently conflicting principles, not least the world-affirming and world-denying aspects of their faith. Is alcoholic refreshment part of the abundant bounty of a loving creator, for which we rightly give thanks, and which is ours to exploit obediently? Or is it essentially evil which it is the Christian's duty to resist and from which he or she hopes to be released?

Biblical Teaching

The biblical writers were well aware of the problems

associated with the irresponsible use of alcohol and, indeed, described some of its ill-effects. However, the general trend of biblical teaching on the matter is reasonably clear. Wine is regarded as one of the fruits of the earth—a gift of God—and its moderate consumption is both pleasurable and acceptable (Psalm 104.14–15, Ecclus. 31.35, John 2.1–11). There is no suggestion in the Bible that alcohol is inherently evil. The dangers of excessive drinking are recognised, however, particularly among those in positions of responsibility, such as priests (Leviticus 10.9) and rulers (Proverbs 31.4–5). The irresponsible use of alcohol impairs the judgement of those in authority. Some groups in Ancient Israel, such as the Nazirites, practised total abstinence (Numbers 6.3, 20) but within Judaism they remain a historical curiosity. In Old and New Testaments alike, therefore, the disciplined use of alcohol is good while its misuse is regarded as sinful.

But biblical teaching has far wider implications for the problems of alcohol misuse than the commonsense conclusions of particular texts. For that is to treat the problem purely as an individual affair. The whole thrust of biblical teaching, however, is towards the growth to wholeness and dignity of the human personality in community, or in communion. The love of God and the love of neighbour are inextricably bound together and fallen humanity is redeemed through the death and ultimate vindication of the one who shows in a unique way how those two aspects of love come together. In other words, alcohol misuse—like any other moral or ethical problem—is not simply an individual matter, to be resolved by the healing or forgiving of particular persons.

It is also a social problem, which affects all of us, because we have a responsibility for each other, and especially those who find it difficult to cope with the pressures of our society. This is part of what the language of the Kingdom of God in the Bible is about. Our actions have consequences; they affect the lives of other people and the life of the community in which we live. If we are truly to 'be members one of another' (Ephesians 4.25) we need to give the social dimension a higher priority in our thinking. This should lead to action on the whole range of social issues which face us. The God who is seen in the Bible as Creator and

Redeemer is also concerned with justice, with the relationships which exist among his people. Exploitation and lack of concern are not part of his wish for us.

Societies which do not exhibit the just and loving relationships which are the signs of the Kingdom are under God's judgement. This is the message contained in almost every kind of biblical writing, from the historical narrative and prophecy through to the words of the Magnificat. Such societies fall short of the mark and may be described as sinful. Their falling short may involve religious idolatry, political ineptitude, or social injustice—every aspect of life in the community is seen to be important to God.

It is in this context that the use and misuse of alcohol has to be seen. The biblical evidence does not support the conclusions that alcohol consumption is 'intrinsically evil'. However, the misuse of alcohol has important consequences not just for the individual but also the community as a whole. It is for this reason that excessive drinking is regarded as contrary to God's laws.

Religious Attitudes to Alcohol

During the Middle Ages, alcohol was part of the staple diet—wine for the wealthy, various kinds of ale, cider, and perry for the poor. Sundays and other holy days gave ordinary people the opportunity to escape from the grinding labour of everyday existence. Not surprisingly this came to be a point of friction between churches and their congregations: medieval and early modern ecclesiastical and judicial records abound with complaints of drunkenness on Sundays—the tavern would open at the end of Mass—and the consequent decline in church attendance in the evening.

It was between about 1500 and 1800, however, that alcohol abuse came to be a serious social problem. The sixteenth century saw the widespread production of brandy—which had been made for medicinal purposes since the twelfth century—and other distilled spirits. The production of alcohol became a profitable business, especially when improved techniques of distillation in the eighteenth century lowered the costs of producing spirits. The state, too, was able to profit through licensing and taxation, as well as the establishment of state monopolies. The expansion of European civilisation into other parts of the globe during this period brought the introduction of other alcoholic drinks, such as rum from the West Indies.

By the eighteenth century, Europe had discovered in alcohol an everyday 'stimulant' and cheap source of calories, easily accessible, a way of making a hard life 'appear momentarily tolerable'. Alcohol was now big business and also had lethal consequences, as the poor of London discovered during the Gin Craze of the 1720s, immortalised in Hogarth's prints. Yet at no time, until the nineteenth century, was there a significant attempt by Christians to press for total abstinence as an appropriate response.

Christianity has always had an ascetic tradition within which total abstinence has been practised, but the consumption of alcohol was usual in most monastic orders. Other Christians—some small sects and some Quakers—abstained from alcohol as one form of luxury. But there was no condemnation of alcohol as evil in itself. The reasons for this can be found in part in a faithful reflection of biblical teaching, in part on the social context in which drinking took place (there were very few alternatives, especially where there was no safe drinking water), and in part on a perception of alcohol misuse as a sin or weakness, to be rectified by the reformation of the individual.

It was not until the end of the eighteenth century that the problem of alcohol misuse began to be subjected to sustained medical and scientific investigation. Benjamin Rush's American study 'Inquiry into the Effects of Ardent Spirits on the Human Mind and Body' was a pioneering attempt to study the effect of alcohol on human physiology and psychology. The findings of Rush and others on the addictive properties of alcohol were one element in the growth of the movement advocating temperance as a response to the rampant alcohol misuse then evident in Britain and America.

In Britain, the Temperance Movement was triggered by the Sale of Beer Act in 1830; in America the movement began a few years earlier. Starting as a coalition of total abstainers and those who urged moderation in drinking, the British Temperance Movement soon split, with the moderates no match for the hardliners—the teetotallers who signed the pledge.

Gradually the Temperance Movement became more

religious and more respectable, a movement for the like-minded rather than an active caring agency. Moreover, it became more religious in a denominational way. The early teetotal speakers had been heckled by Wesleyans but by the 1870s and 1880s Methodists, Baptists, and, eventually, the Salvation Army had been largely won over to the cause. Temperance had become a respectable cause with strong political overtones, yearning for the prohibition which would solve the problems of British society. As such it was too partisan to be able to pioneer the broader approach to alcohol misuse which the situation demanded—the need for co-operation with all who were concerned about the problem, whatever their religious beliefs.

The shorter opening hours and higher taxes introduced during the First World War were the closest the Temperance Movement in Britain came to Prohibition. In America, where the Movement had a higher political profile, Prohibition was enforced between 1919 and 1932. It was not, however, the panacea for which its advocates had hoped. By the 1930s Temperance was no longer the force it had been and the various organisations dedicated to total abstinence have lost much of their influence.

The Christian Way Forward

We have seen that the biblical writings, taken as a whole, have direct and relevant things to say about social issues in general. How may these be applied to the serious issue of alcohol misuse?

It is important to be clear that alcohol misuse is not a simple problem admitting of a straightforward solution. The mistake made by many campaigning organisations is to assume that this is the case. This enables them to aim at a single, easily communicable goal, such as Prohibition, which will solve the problem once and for all.

However, the problem of alcohol misuse is a complex issue, involving questions of medical treatment for addiction, personal responsibility and motivation, and the social conditions in which alcohol misuse takes place. In a society in which drinking is socially acceptable—and often socially required—even a moderate increase in overall drinking has a disproportionate effect on the number of people who are put at risk from alcohol-related problems. The informal social constraints upon which a balanced Christian view of the use of alcohol depended are no longer strong. We rely on alcohol to a greater extent than we care to admit.

It is instructive to compare the approach of the other great monotheistic religions in this matter. Both Judaism and Islam start, like Christianity, from the understanding that wine is good in itself but the two religious traditions have taken very different routes from this starting point. Jewish law and tradition prescribes the consumption of wine—by both adults and children—on most religious and social occasions, especially at Passover, on the Sabbath, and at all major religious festivals. Wine therefore has an important, almost sacramental, place in Jewish life and tradition. By giving alcohol such an exalted place, Jews have never experienced its misuse to the extent that it is found in other social groups, and a Jewish movement for total abstinence would be unthinkable. If you respect and value something you are more likely to use it responsibly.

In Islam, on the other hand, the consequences of the misuse of alcohol in the Arab peninsula during the pre-Islamic period led to the total prohibition, even for medical purposes, which is still in force in the Arab world today. There are passages in the Qur'an which suggest that it is the abuse of alcohol rather than alcohol itself which is wrong, but the effect of alcohol in dulling the intellect and senses is sufficient to cause its ban from a religious tradition in which the clarity of the will and of one's intentions are given paramount importance.

In both Judaism and Islam, therefore, teaching on alcohol reflects the broader cultural and social setting of those religions and the kinds of relationship and authority structures which exist within them. Because they have been historically more clearly socially defined than Christianity, they have been able to continue their traditional teaching into the modern world.

Christian teaching also reflects its context, but because the social cohesion of Christianity has become so fragmented over the past two or three hundred years there has been confusion and imprecision in much Christian ethical instruction. Today this is reflected in the different approaches to alcohol abuse in various Christian denominations. Some denominations ban the use of alcohol on their property but even the Methodist Church, long at the forefront of the Temperance Movement, lifted the ban on ministers' houses in 1977, recognising that total abstinence was no longer an enforceable view. Other churches, such as the Episcopal Church in the United States, have set up caring agencies and asked their dioceses to adopt policies regulating local responses to alcohol misuse, such as the reduction of the prominence of alcohol at church functions.

Such steps are a recognition that the handling of alcohol misuse is an issue which involves all of us. It is not just a matter for specialist helpers and those who suffer from misuse. But the Christian way forward is not an isolated or exclusive approach. It seeks to co-operate with all agencies which have special skills and insights to offer in making people whole, which is God's wish for all of his people, not just believers. Within this broadly based approach there are Christian insights as well as responsibilities which need to be given their place.

These include:

(i) The recognition that each individual is uniquely valued by God, who desires that they may be made whole and brought to fullness of life.

(ii) The recognition that helping people in this way is not just a medical matter but requires ministry to the different aspects of the personality. We have to deal with the feelings of guilt and inadequacy, both in the individual and among his or her family or friends. We need to provide intelligent and realistic support, especially at times when the sense of failure seems overwhelming.

(iii) The recognition that such healing and reconciliation is needed by all of us; that the misuse of alcohol is a symptom of the state of the society in which we live.

(iv) The recognition that the Church has a prophetic role in these circumstances. It has a responsibility for the spiritual well-being of all people and the duty of bearing Christian witness to society as a whole.

No Christian response to a problem such as alcohol misuse can simply be the putting of theory into practice. We look to the Christian tradition, and especially to the Bible, for the general approach—the 'style' almost—of our response and allow that teaching to interpret and be interpreted by our experience and the actual situations in which we find ourselves. Our response needs to be both positive and realistic and, in the next chapter, we shall go on to consider the practical implications of exercising Christian responsibility in responding to drinking problems.

4

RESPONDING TO DRINKING PROBLEMS

Having discussed some of the Christian principles and responsibilities in responding to alcohol problems in the last chapter, we now go on to look in some detail at a practical response to individual problem drinkers. At the outset, we need to draw some distinction between a drink-related problem and a problem drinker.

A parish priest may conduct the funeral of the victim of a drunken driver, comforting the bereaved family and counselling them out of anger and bitterness and into forgiveness and peace. That is part of the Church's everyday response to alcohol misuse and requires some specialist knowledge and insight. A church member may go over the top in one night of drunken revelry, end up in court the next day and require pastoral support to overcome his shame and discomfort. This is an example of alcohol misuse but the misuser, although 'at risk', is not necessarily a problem drinker. A young girl in the parish may drink too much at a party, end up having sexual intercourse with a stranger, and become pregnant. She will bear the consequences of her actions for the rest of her life and require considerable practical and spiritual support but without being classified as a problem drinker.

So there are a catalogue of drink-related incidences which receive the attention of pastoral workers, but this chapter will be concerned with just two groups of people. The first is the person who regularly gets into difficulty with alcohol and/or who is drinking consistently at harmful levels. The second is the relative or close acquaintance of such a person whose life is influenced by their behaviour.

Identifying the Problem Drinker

If you adopt a traditional view of alcohol misuse, your task is simple. You are looking for a person who is at rock bottom, whose life has been devastated by drinking, who drinks at every opportunity and hides bottles everywhere. Friends and relatives are alienated, financial resources have dwindled and debts have mounted, and all responsibilities are neglected. This person experiences blackouts and fits, shaking violently until the first drink of the day is gulped down. This caricature is all too real to some people because we do come across men and women who fit this picture.

The question is—Would such a person's problem have been identified five years ago? or ten years ago? or twenty years ago? The difficulty has been that the problem drinkers who are easiest to spot are at a stage when they are the most difficult to help. The earlier the problem is identified, the easier it will be to overcome. Greater stress is now being placed on the early identification of problem drinkers. The chapters which follow will illuminate this further.

One of the problems with the caricature outlined above is that if this is the picture of a drinking problem, which is fixed in many people's minds, they will tend to say things like 'My husband can't have a drink problem because he still gives me housekeeping money,' or 'I don't have a drink problem because I don't drink every day and I never have blackouts.'

What then are the first symptoms of a developing drinking problem? A number of helpful questionnaires have been produced which contain the appropriate questions to ask. An example is reproduced in Figure 5.

Broadly speaking, people develop drinking problems because their use of alcohol is inappropriate. In simple terms,

They drink too much
or They drink for the wrong reasons.

Whatever the origins, the problem drinker normally ends up experiencing both forms of misuse. The limits mentioned in Chapter 1 are exceeded and they drink for relief of anxiety and pressure or to escape from responsibility and conflict.

Identifying inappropriate use or spotting the early symptoms is an important first step, but such insight is useless unless it can be applied to and received by the individual.

Challenging the Problem Drinker

It should not be assumed that all drinking excesses result in someone becoming a problem drinker. If that was the case, the majority of the population would be in need of help. It is part of normal human behaviour to take risks from time to time and to push the limits of all pleasurable experiences. It is a normal part of growing up for young people to test out their capacity for alcohol. Certainly, Christians must condemn unacceptable drinking behaviour (e.g. drunken driving), but we must be careful not to over-react to less dangerous drinking practices. We risk alienating those in greatest need of help if we adopt too rigid a position.

While there is a need for caution, we need not go to the other extreme and avoid any form of challenge until the person concerned is 'at rock bottom' and desperate for help. There will be opportunities to engage a problem drinker in positive discussion before he or she is at the end of the road, and we need to take advantage of those opportunities or it may be too late.

Coupled with the belief that problem drinkers need to reach the bottom before they can reach up is the related notion that 'all problem drinkers are liars'. This has some foundation because the strong tendency is to deny there is a problem and to cover it up in any way possible. However, the question is whether the responses of problem drinkers to their condition are any different from the basic tendencies which we all experience in the wake of personal traumas.

Pause for a moment and reflect on an event in your life when you made a big mistake, where you lost control or had an accident. What were the first thoughts which entered your mind? 'How do I get out of this one?' or 'Who or what can I blame?' or 'No, it can't have happened!' or 'I didn't

FIGURE 5

Alcohol Problem Questionnaire

During the last few months		
Have you resolved to cut down your drinking but been unable to make any changes?	YES	NO
Has anyone close to you expressed concern about the level of your drinking?	YES	NO
Has your work been in any way affected by your drinking?	YES	NO
Have you lied to anyone about your drinking?	YES	NO
Have you used alcohol as a substitute for food?	YES	NO
Have you ever been surprised at the amount you have spent on alcohol?	YES	NO
Have you been unusually aggressive after drinking?	YES	NO
Have you been in trouble with the police as a result of your drinking?	YES	NO
Have you been unable to recall what you did during a drinking bout?	YES	NO
Have you felt shaky the morning after a bout?	YES	NO
Have you been drunk on two successive days?	YES	NO
Have you had a drink first thing in the morning to 'calm your nerves'?	YES	NO
Have you needed a drink before facing a difficult situation?	YES	NO
Have you felt guilty about your drinking?	YES	NO
Have you given up any sports, hobbies or other leisure interests because of your drinking?	YES	NO
Have you felt that you have been losing control of your drinking?	YES	NO
Have you suffered any illness as a result of your drinking?	YES	NO
Have you experienced any sexual difficulties as a result of your drinking?	YES	NO
Have you ever planned your day around when and where you can get drink?	YES	NO

If you have answered YES to any question, you are having problems with your drinking. You need to think about cutting down and you may need help to do so.

really knock over that priceless vase, it was a freak gust of wind!'

It seems that what we confront in problem drinkers is no more nor less than normal human emotions and reactions. Consider what we are asking of someone when we press them to admit they have a drinking problem. One of our most positive human experiences is a sense of 'being in control'. For example, we plan what we want to do on a particular day, we go out and do it and we are satisfied. Admitting to a drink problem is to say, 'I have lost control of a bit of my life, I might intend to stop at two pints but I go on to ten.' It seems easier to say, 'Sure, I had ten pints, what of it? I can handle it.' Accompanying this natural denial is the stigma attached to drunkenness. The drunk is often a figure of fun and an object of derision. For a woman, the shame is multiplied. To challenge effectively, we need to communicate an accurate picture of problem drinking.

So there are barriers to be overcome if the problem drinker is to be challenged at an early stage. There are no easy answers to this dilemma. Leaving leaflets around in the hope that the person will pick one up and see the light is mere wishful thinking and can generate an undercurrent of suspicion and distrust. So what does work? An effective approach for one person would be totally inappropriate for another. However, the longer someone takes to face up to the problem, the more difficult recovery will be.

Ideally, the person closest to the problem drinker should speak directly to them and express their concerns. However, it often happens that members of the family are too caught up in the emotions of the situation to cope with confrontation. A parish priest, helpful outsider or a friend of the same sex may be able to make the breakthrough. Alternatively, a word from the family G.P. may be effective.

The best time to challenge the problem drinker is just after a drink-related event. For example, an accident or a family row or the onset of a related physical complaint or a crisis at work would provide opportunities. It is best to avoid any confrontations when the person is intoxicated.

If the problem drinker accepts there is a problem, the next step is to consider the various options for action.

Helping the Problem Drinker

It should be stressed that there are a wide range of options available for the problem drinker seeking help. Resolving a drink problem does not necessarily involve contact with professional specialists. Christians need to be aware that self-help guides are available in book or pamphlet format (see Appendix B). They are targeted at those who acknowledge that they are drinking too much, who want to change and to enjoy alcohol in a way that is not harmful, but who are not physically dependent. Of themselves or as an accompaniment to personal counselling, these self-help manuals are proving very useful. However, the desire to seek professional help (even if as a last resort) would evidence a strong commitment to change. The following chapter lists all the forms of specialist help available with advice on how to get in touch.

Whatever other forms of help are being used, the support of family, friends and colleagues is crucial to recovery. In a church situation, specific accountability to a designated person may provide an important reference point for the person who finds that the resolution of their drinking problem involves good weeks and bad weeks. The objective perspective of a third person can help them maintain a positive view of their overall progress.

Successful recovery involves engaging the problem drinker in reconciling their past to their present and developing an effective strategy for the future. Let's consider this in some detail.

(a) *Understanding the Past*

To have confidence that any problem will be resolved, its origins need to be clearly understood. Of course, the concept of 'alcoholism' as a 'sickness' would make any exploration of the past irrelevant for 'People do not become alcoholics, they are born alcoholics'. However, if we reject this view, we have to help people reflect on their past use of alcohol. One practical way of doing this is to encourage the person to draw a 'road map' of their life, reflecting on significant milestones or crossroads and focusing on accompanying changes in their pattern of alcohol consumption.

FIGURE 6

Mary's Lifestory

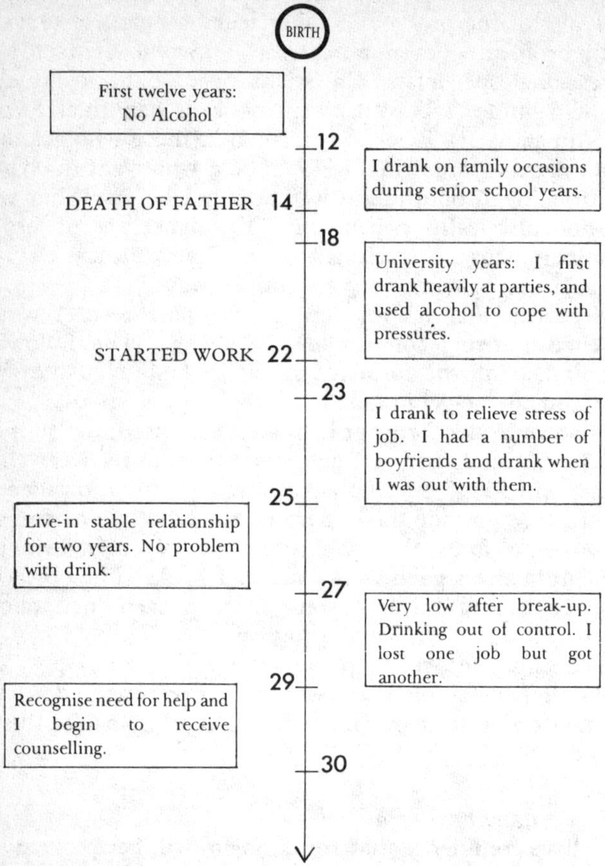

In the illustration (Figure 6), the woman drank very occasionally until she left home to attend university. She coped with the pressures of a strange environment by bolstering her confidence with alcohol. She therefore *learned* to use alcohol to relieve her anxieties. There were alternative ways of coping but she *chose* alcohol and its use then dominated her growing experiences. Consequently, in adult life, she continued to *choose* alcohol to relieve life's pressures because she had not *learned* any alternative coping strategies.

(b) *Coping with the Present*

Whatever the underlying problems which might have contributed to the alcohol problem, it is a problem in itself and practical steps must be taken to avoid further misuse and damage.

Any physical damage caused by previous excesses must be acknowledged. Anyone with any doubts about their physical condition or fears about the symptoms of detoxification should see their doctor. Some may be advised never to drink again because of damage to vital organs. Others may be in such an unstable mental or emotional state that it would be unreasonable to think about resuming drinking for the foreseeable future. Some problem drinkers may simply have to acknowledge that alcohol is not right for them and never will be. However, there are those who will be determined to continue drinking and some will be able to achieve the goal of controlled drinking. While each problem drinker has to choose for themselves whether they will drink again or not, the best advice for all would be to have a few alcohol-free weeks at the very least.

For those who choose to resume drinking immediately or at a later stage, an analysis must be made of the recent drinking pattern and steps taken to change it. One of the most effective disciplines in this respect is to keep a drinking diary. Even if the person is resolved not to drink, at least for a short period, some form of diary is useful to help them identify the times when they feel most vulnerable (an example is given in Figure 7). After keeping a diary for a week or two the person should be in a position to identify the times when they are most 'at risk' and plan their personal strategy accordingly. Reasonable limits should be set and some personal rules adopted. For example, a 'cut-off' point for daily consumption should be set (i.e. a man might determine never to drink more than six units of alcohol in a single day; a comparative limit for a woman would be four). Following the setting of reasonable targets, a diary should be kept for about twelve weeks so that progress can be carefully monitored.

If the problem drinker cannot keep within agreed targets, then they should be prepared to review their drinking goals and possibly opt for total abstinence as the safest way forward.

FIGURE 7

Drinking Diary

Day	Time	Who with and where?	What drinks?	Consequences	Cost	Units
Monday						
Tuesday						
Wednesday						
Thursday						
Friday						
Saturday						
Sunday						
Week ending			Total for week			

(c) *Facing the Future*

The problem drinker should be encouraged to take time before making any long-term decisions. Rash promises should be discouraged as they may be regretted later. The natural tendency is to want to sort out everything overnight but real change will take time. Many have lived with the thought that 'if only I get my drinking under control, everything will be all right' before they finally seek help. The reality is that there are no shortcuts, particularly with relationships. Trust can be lost very easily. It takes time to rebuild.

If, as in the above example, there is a tendency to use alcohol in the face of pressure, alternative coping strategies must be worked out. If not, what will the person turn to if the only way they know of coping is drinking. For the person with a growing Christian faith there are obvious alternatives in prayer and fellowship. For some, alcohol has taken up a lot of their time, energy and money. They will soon be bored if they do not find acceptable alternative outlets. They will need encouragement to persevere with these strategies as their concentration will not be what it was.

Although physical detoxification from the effects of alcohol is usually experienced within a matter of days, the mental effects take much longer to reverse. A sense of low self-esteem and feelings of overwhelming guilt may persist for some time. These feelings can provoke thoughts like 'Why bother?', 'What's the point?', 'Who cares anyway?', 'I'm giving up!', 'It'll never work out!' This sort of outlook obviously mitigates against sustained recovery through difficult patches. It helps if the person appreciates that full recovery does not happen quickly and that they can look forward to a happier outlook in the course of time.

The above perspective should be helpful for Christians (or indeed anyone else) who are in contact with a problem drinker. However, for some problem drinkers, the challenge to look at their past and to face a future without alcohol is more threatening than it is promising. Consider the plight of a woman who has discovered that alcohol can dull the painful memories of childhood abuse. She will not easily give up alcohol or readily explore the reasons for her drinking. It is to such that the Christian ministry of reconciliation is especially appropriate and those who counsel them require great patience and compassion.

However, it is often those closest to the problem who have greatest difficulty in seeing a way out. We will conclude this chapter with a look at the needs of relatives.

Living With a Problem Drinker

There can be few more distressing experiences than to watch someone you love deteriorate mentally and physically with the consequences of self-inflicted abuse. As mentioned above, the normal human reaction is to deny that anything is happening and hope that it will just go away. It is also normal for relatives, close friends and colleagues to try and cover up for him or her. This collusion serves to shield the problem drinker from the consequences of his or her actions and effectively puts off the time when the reality of the problem is faced.

Moreover, subtle but destructive changes are taking place in the fabric of relationships as loving acts are squandered and trust is broken. Threats and promises may be exchanged between husband and wife but neither are kept. 'If you drink again, I'll leave you!' says one. 'I'll never touch another drop!' says the other but neither stick to what they say. Consequently, mutual respect is lost. With a strong sense of duty, the sober partner stretches love to the limit and beyond. Eventually, there is a breaking point when love and acceptance can be suddenly replaced by hatred and rejection. The end, for some marriages, is messy and leaves a bitter taste for years to come. Yet, much of this pain could be alleviated if the problem is confronted at an early stage and the sober partner refuses to collude with the other's unreality.

The families of problem drinkers need as much help as the problem drinker and should be fully engaged in the recovery process. When the problem drinker is not actively seeking help, the family's need for support is even greater (the appropriate forms of help for families are also referred to in Chapter 5).

The damage to children should not be underestimated. Again, the danger is that the parents would want to gloss over the effects on the children. It is easier to deny their difficulties than to face up to them and help them. In the United States, there is a great emphasis on services for the children of problem drinkers which is lacking in Britain. There is evidence to suggest that the children of problem drinkers are more likely to develop problems than the children of normal drinkers. Without good adult models of sensible drinking behaviour they are not likely to handle alcohol themselves with any confidence. It is vital that the children are given an opportunity to express their feelings and resolve some of the pains, fears and anxieties which might otherwise plague their adult life.

The starting point for families is to see that love can be tough. It is not unloving to allow someone to endure the consequences of their actions. At the first sign of a developing problem, the limits must be set. If a teenager is sick after a drinks party or wets the bed in a drunken stupor, let them clean up the mess. If a spouse with a hangover requests that someone should call the office to report sickness, let them do it themselves. If the bus fare is spent on drink, let them walk to work. Are these actions unloving? No, for they represent a love which sees that the alternative is far harsher in the long term. So it is not unloving to refuse to buy someone a drink or to give them money to do so. Ultimately, it would not be unloving to abandon a drunken and violent spouse both for the sake of any children and for the sake of the problem drinker who, if unchecked, may have to carry an increasingly crippling burden of guilt. The courage of the individual who has to choose separation should be matched by the church. While Christians would not wish to be seen to be encouraging the break-up of a marriage, the offer of a 'safe house' would seem to be a legitimate caring response in such circumstances.

Christian counsellors and pastoral workers, who strive to exercise a ministry of reconciliation, should not underestimate the depths of emotional pain and scarring which an alcohol problem generates within a family. Reconciliation, if at all possible, will not be gained easily or cheaply.

5

THE HELPING SERVICES

Very few of the many specialist services currently available for problem drinkers in Britain were in existence thirty years ago. Then, although the condition of 'alcoholism' was recognised, very few doctors considered sufferers to be worthy of much attention and the government did not have alcohol on its agenda. Only those enduring the traumas of detoxification could expect intensive treatment and that would only be provided in a mental hospital. A network of Alcoholics Anonymous groups was beginning to develop but alternative community-based support was virtually non-existent.

Consequently, many of the services described in this chapter are relatively new. For some, the value of their work and/or the validity of their treatment philosophies and practices is still subject to rigorous appraisal. It should not be assumed that agencies with similar labels offer similar services. Neither the network of NHS Alcohol Treatment Units, nor the network of local alcohol advisory services, are subject to any uniform guidelines for service provision. Even the self-help groups in the fellowship of Alcoholics Anonymous, while all adhering to the same basic principles, are in some aspects as variable as the people who participate in them.

We will begin by discussing certain trends in service development and go on to list the various forms of help available along with some practical guidelines regarding access to the agencies described. This will provide both clergy and laity with some basic information which we hope will be useful in assessing the needs of problem drinkers and their families.

Recent Trends

The development of alcohol services has been greatly influenced by changes in perception of the nature of the problem. The dominance of the 'disease concept' in alcohol studies has been steadily declining over the past two decades, although it is now experiencing a resurgence in some quarters, particularly in the private sector, where a number of new treatment units are run on American models. While some may have reservations about the private sector's contribution, these innovations have had the effect of increasing the range of choices available to individuals.

In terms of medical care for problem drinkers, one of the most significant changes in recent years has been in the management of detoxification. The traditional image of the alcohol misuser embraces all the horrors of shakes, delirium tremens (D.T.s), fits, and so on. However, the reality is that very few problem drinkers are familiar with these experiences. Most heavy drinkers can come off alcohol with the minimum of medical supervision. Where some drug therapy is advisable, it usually only amounts to reducing doses of common tranquillisers over about seven to ten days at the most. Of course, there are still some chronic cases whose lives would be at risk without specialist medical intervention.

Within the NHS, 'Care in the Community' has been the banner under which radical changes in psychiatric services have been taking place. Small community-based units are favoured as the unwieldy mental institutions of a past era are progressively dismantled. Consequently, opportunities for in-patient care for the detoxification and rehabilitation of problem drinkers are diminishing. While some write off these changes as a cost-cutting exercise, they have happily coincided with a growing conviction that alcohol problems are best treated in the context of their associated relationships and pressures (i.e. in the community). The danger is that this process will go too far and those who have a genuine need for special care and respite from the community will have no places left in the NHS.

Nevertheless, awareness of alcohol problems at the level of primary medical care has been significantly heightened.

G.P.s, Health Visitors, and District Nurses are now encouraged to identify alcohol problems at an early stage and are making successful interventions. In some localities, the primary care personnel are backed up by a community alcohol team, representing a growing NHS commitment to tackle alcohol misuse before specialist treatment is required. The local G.P. remains, for many, the first source of help with a drinking problem.

For those who, for a number of reasons, prefer not to take their problems to statutory agencies, the voluntary sector offers a range of services and has often been at the forefront of promoting innovative forms of help. Nevertheless, many voluntary agencies struggle to raise the necessary income each year and are finding themselves to be more and more in competition with statutory services for a share of public and private funds. Consequently, there is little certainty around concerning future service provision and the strain on services is only likely to be alleviated by a significant injection of central government funds. The recent release of such funds to build up a network of drugs services was very welcome but, looking at the two problems in perspective, it seems that alcohol misuse merits the greater attention.

Be that as it may, it is important that Christians should be aware of the variety of services currently on offer in most parts of the country. While most space will be given to specialist services, non-specialist forms of help are equally important and are also mentioned.

A. Statutory Services

Primary Medical Care

G.P.s, along with district nursing staff, can offer advice, treatment and support to problem drinkers. Where extra help is required, the G.P. can refer on to specialist district-based services.

District Psychiatric Services

Psychiatrists and psychologists accept referrals of problem drinkers from G.P.s and offer a range of services including in-patient detoxification, out-patient appointments, day-care units, home visits, group therapy, etc.

Community Alcohol Teams

In 1978, the Kessel report[1] (of a government committee set up to investigate the provision of alcohol services) made a number of recommendations about local developments. One of their suggestions, which has been taken up in a number of areas, was to set up multi-disciplinary Community Alcohol Teams (CATs) with representation from Health, Social Services, and Voluntary Agency personnel. There are now about fourteen projects with a number of others in the planning stage.

Most teams function by using the time of seconded specialist staff on a sessional basis (e.g. a Consultant Psychiatrist might give half a day each week) as well as by employing a few full-time workers. A typical team might include community psychiatric nurses, a psychologist and/or psychiatrist (part-time), a social worker and/or probation officer (perhaps part-time), counsellors and administrative/clerical staff. Most teams offer a consultancy service to primary care workers as well as dealing with direct referrals. With respect to detoxification, they tend to offer treatment at home with domiciliary visits as back-up but have reasonable access to acute psychiatric beds whenever necessary.

The great value of these teams is that they represent a co-ordinated approach employing the skills and experience of all the relevant statutory and voluntary services. In some localities the CAT's role is very similar to that of a local alcohol advisory service. Many of these teams will be known as Community Alcohol and Drug Teams or Community Addiction Teams although some CATs just confine themselves to problems associated with alcohol misuse.

Most Community Alcohol Teams are easily accessible, either directly in response to local publicity or by referral on from primary care workers (i.e. G.P., Health Visitor, Social Worker, etc.).

Alcoholism Treatment Units

The first National Health Service special treatment unit was established at Warlingham Park Hospital, near Croydon, in the early 1950s. The success of this unit convinced the NHS that the treatment of alcohol dependency was one of its legitimate responsibilities. In 1962, a circular was issued which recommended the development of Alcoholism Treatment Units (ATUs) in each Health Region. At one time, there were thirty ATUs across the country but, more recently, some have closed down and others are under threat. These units have traditionally concentrated on the severely dependent problem drinker and have offered a detoxification programme followed by a variety of therapies to facilitate rehabilitation. Whereas local acute psychiatric units have sometimes been restricted to offering detoxification only, the regional units have been able to offer a treatment regime lasting as long as two months.

As earlier interventions into alcohol problems have been developed, there has been less and less commitment to in-patient care as a cost-effective form of treatment. Consequently, some ATUs have been developed as regional resource units with close links with community services and an increased profile in research and education. It is considered that the complete elimination of specialist in-patient facilities would be undesirable as there remain many problem drinkers who, because of acute social or physical disabilities, do benefit from more intensive forms of therapy.

Access to these units is normally through local medical and psychiatric services but some have an open admissions policy and can be contacted directly by potential patients and/or their relatives.

Non-Medical Services

Social workers and probation officers have a good working knowledge of alcohol problems and can provide relevant support. Some non-medical services provide special support for problem drinkers. For example, many probation offices run education and/or therapy groups. Staff in non-specialist day centres and hotels often have great experience in dealing with alcohol problems.

B. Non-Statutory Services

Alcohol Advisory Services

In the last twenty-five years a network of Local Councils on Alcoholism has been developed across the country. These are local independent voluntary bodies with a special concern for establishing accessible information and counselling services in each centre of population. Their development was co-ordinated centrally by the National Council on Alcoholism up until 1983 when its activities were merged into a new national body, Alcohol Concern. The size of these agencies varies. Some are regional bodies which cover a whole health region and employ a large staff in a variety of projects. Some may only cover one health district and be run with just one full-time officer or a small group of volunteers. It follows that their range of activities also varies. Their common goals can be identified as follows:

(a) the provision of information and counselling for problem drinkers and their friends or relatives;
(b) the monitoring of alcohol misuse at a local level and providing information for the media, the public, and statutory services;
(c) the provision of education and training for primary care staff and other relevant professional workers;
(d) co-ordinating local responses to alcohol misuse;
(e) planning and developing local prevention strategies;
(f) promoting/initiating new services and projects.

There are now about seventy such services in England and Wales, including twenty in the Greater London area. They qualify for 'pump-priming' money which the DHSS channel through Alcohol Concern but, once established, they are totally dependent on local sources of funding, mainly Health and Local Authority grants. Their services are free and confidential. Recent statistics suggest that they are responding to an increasing number of enquiries each year. As well as counselling services, some of which involve trained volunteers, the largest of these local services are involved in running day centres, clubs, and residential facilities.

In recent years, the growing emphasis on drugs problems has led to some of these agencies becoming Local Councils on Addiction and taking on all forms of substance abuse. There is no evidence to suggest that this has had any adverse effect on clients' readiness to ask for help.

Local counselling and information services are usually well publicised. Look in alphabetical phone books under Alcoholism or 'Anytown' Alcohol Advisory Service, or in the appropriate section at the front of Thompson's or Yellow Pages. Local G.P.s should also be familiar with these services. Whatever the particular service need of a problem drinker, these agencies are a useful first point of contact as they are normally in touch with all the relevant services in their locality and will also have information on the national help network. Alcohol Concern publishes a national directory of alcohol services and can provide information on all local agencies (see Appendix C).

Homeless Services

Many services for problem drinkers were developed in response to the particular needs of the homeless or 'skid row' alcoholic. For them, rehabilitation was as much associated with the provision of therapeutic accommodation as it was with advice and counselling. There are about seventy-five therapeutic hostels in England and Wales, most of which have been established by voluntary bodies. In addition, there are about twenty-six day centres, most of them in inner cities. Many of these projects have close links with the Church and some are run on Christian principles and provide opportunities for Christian education and worship. Ideally, these projects are able to offer a range of accommodation from basic shelter to hostels, half-way houses, and independent flats.

Traditionally, access to these services is conditional upon being homeless and being committed to staying 'dry' but there is a growing emphasis on the provision of 'short-stay' accommodation for those who may simply need some 'time out' from the pressures of their home environment.

Access to the most basic of these facilities is on a drop-in basis but, for some placements, there will be a waiting period during which an assessment will be made of the potential resident. Any alcohol advisory service should have information on local facilities.

Self-Help Groups

Alcoholics Anonymous (commonly known as AA) is an organisation of men and women with the common goal of stopping drinking and staying dry. They are committed purely to mutual support and do not engage in public campaigns or have any formal links with any other body.

Although each group is independent they all adhere to common principles and a common twelve-step programme.

In most people's minds, there is an automatic association between drinking problems and AA, and many medical and psychiatric services use AA as their first choice of referral when confronted with an 'alcoholic' patient. There are over 1,000 local groups in the U.K. and this network ensures that, in every town, there is likely to be at least a contact person for AA. In large centres of population, there is likely to be an AA meeting every night of the week. Some of these meetings are publicised as 'open' so anyone can go along.

AA members have a strong commitment to helping others and are prepared to turn out day or night to help each other and meet new members. They have been described as a quasi-religious body because each member is encouraged to put their trust in 'a higher power', whatever they might conceive that higher power to be. For some, there is something mystical in the fellowship of AA and, for those who are also Church members, their higher power is a personal faith in God.

For those problem drinkers who are convinced that they are dependent on alcohol and need to stop altogether, AA provides a very effective approach. For those whose problems are less severe or whose alcohol use is tied in with underlying social and emotional disorders, AA can be inappropriate. AA's belief with respect to returning to normal social drinking is that one drink will lead to another and another and so on. For those who are not ready for total abstinence, this can be a self-fulfilling prophecy as that first drink will inevitably make them feel very uncomfortable and anxious. AA's value should not be underestimated but its programme will not work for all types of problem drinker.

Two other self-help organisations have close links with AA and share the same understanding that alcoholism is a sickness. These are Al Anon, for the relatives of alcoholics, and Al Ateen for the children. As with AA, these groups provide invaluable caring support.

A contact number is available in most telephone directories. The Samaritans maintain lists of local members who can be contacted. The national service offices can also be contacted for local details (see Appendix C). If in any doubt about the appropriateness of putting any problem drinker in touch with AA, the local alcohol advisory service would be the preferred point of contact as they can provide information on a range of options as well as introducing enquirers to AA.

A relatively new development in self-help has been the organisation, 'Drinkwatchers'. Their groups are run on similar lines to 'Weightwatchers' and focus on cutting down rather than on cutting out. Some local alcohol advisory services facilitate groups which are run on similar principles so they might be a good first point of contact. Alternatively, there is a national number to call (see Appendix C).

Other Voluntary Agencies

Samaritans, Marriage Guidance Councils, Citizens Advice Bureaux, Cruse, Age Concern, are all local voluntary services which encounter problem drinking clients from time to time. Those which offer counselling may be able to offer support but most, while meeting basic practical needs and responding to the current crisis, will refer on to appropriate specialist help.

C. The Private Sector

The growth in private medicine has included the provision of alcohol services. Some Health Insurance schemes allow for this type of care. Like the public and voluntary sectors, there is a mix of treatment philosophies around which determine the type of care on offer. Some treatment regimes, which have been tried and tested in the United States, have been imported here. They are characterised by the understanding that chemical dependency is a sickness. Consequently, these units have close links with AA groups and ex-patients are encouraged to participate in AA when they return home. While some private psychiatric units and nursing homes have been providing alcohol services for many years, the success of some of the newer units has yet to be determined.

Access to private facilities is less straightforward but most local alcohol advisory services should have some information on them. Some units are supported by charitable trusts so 'ability to pay' is not always a condition for admission.

D. Employee Assistance Programmes

A number of major employers have adopted Workplace Alcohol Policies which are designed to facilitate early intervention with problem drinkers whose problem encroaches on their work performance. It is reckoned that the implementation of such schemes can save companies a great deal of money as well as offering individual employees the opportunity to obtain help with their problem. In some cases, the employee would be referred to a local specialist service for treatment and counselling. Some companies have trained welfare staff who can provide appropriate counselling.

Access is by contact with the personnel department of major companies. Under some of these policies, the worker is guaranteed a confidential service if he or she makes the first move.

E. Detoxification Units

In 1971, a Home Office Committee recommended that a system of care and rehabilitation should be provided as an alternative to fines and imprisonment for drunkenness offenders. It proposed the setting up of detoxification centres which would receive offenders who had been apprehended by the police. The DHSS followed up this recommendation and funding was invested in research projects. However, the development of access to such facilities in each centre of population has been largely abandoned. In recent years, the burden on the courts has been lightened by a scheme of cautioning rather than charging drunkenness offenders. The provision of community detoxification units is still a live issue but it is unlikely that the Home Office or DHSS will back any more projects.

Access to such facilities is limited to police referral in the few areas where any provision is made.

Summary

As the above list clearly demonstrates, there are a whole range of options for problem drinkers in this country. This point needs to be got across to those in need of help. The stigma of 'alcoholism', and its associated false images, work against individuals making that big first step and saying, 'I need help.' There is a fear that they will be labelled and shunted down one particular track, possibly to psychiatric care. The reality is refreshingly different. Very few of the services mentioned above would consider their clients to be 'alcoholics'. In the main, they are concerned with offering simple information and counselling for people who could never identify with the 'alcoholic' label.

The one question mark over the services network described is future funding. For too many services in the non-statutory sector, there is a constant uncertainty regarding next year's grants. It is to be hoped that, as our understanding of the nature and extent of the problem matures, there will be a greater public commitment to these services.

Certainly, we are already seeing a greater professional commitment to the needs of problem drinkers across the full spectrum of social and medical services. The view that problem drinkers are very difficult to deal with, and should be referred on to specialists at the first opportunity, is no longer prevalent. It is more often the case that primary care staff, who are responding to many conflicting pressures, simply don't have sufficient time to give to a problem drinker whose complex problems may not unravel without a series of counselling sessions.

The picture then is of growth in awareness, understanding, professional training, and in sources of help. The role of local churches in exercising a caring ministry along with other professional workers is a prime concern. We shall be discussing various ways in which this can be achieved in the final chapter. It suffices here to remark that both lay and ordained pastoral workers are frequently encountering situations in which drink is a major problem. Many offer long-term support to individuals and families but there is also a need for greater awareness amongst clergy and their congregations of the means of preventing drinking problems.

6

PREVENTING DRINKING PROBLEMS

In the third chapter we observed that Christians have historically played a significant part in prevention initiatives, even to the extent of securing national prohibition in the United States. While we would not expect the Church today to endorse the same goal, it can and should address itself to the problems of alcohol misuse in society. However, the Church should not be content simply to respond to the individual problems which are generated by society but should seek to influence and change the social and economic environment which apparently encourages the development of those problems. If successful, the Church will do a great service to future generations of potential problem drinkers.

Prevention can be interpreted in different ways. It is helpful to see prevention as a continuum of care. Care for the gravely ill advanced problem drinker is expressed in providing support and medical care to prevent their untimely death. Care for one who is experiencing the first symptoms of a developing problem is expressed in providing information and counselling to prevent the worst ravages of alcohol abuse ensuing. Care for the teenager about to join the adult drinking world is expressed in providing alcohol education in schools and youth clubs. Care for the whole population is expressed in the promotion of healthy attitudes to drinking.

Whatever prevention initiatives are taken, they must be related to the actual processes of change which can already be observed in the nation's drinking behaviour. Let's now take a look at the principal factors that influence drinking behaviour and the prevalence of alcohol-related problems in our society.

Historical Perspective

Since records began, significant fluctuations in alcohol consumption have been observable from one period of history to another. In the early years of this century, pubs in England and Wales could open for anything up to nineteen and a half hours per day. Restrictions were imposed during the First World War and, by 1918, pub hours in most places were restricted to less than six hours per day. Accompanied by changes in taxation, these restrictions reduced consumption by about 60 per cent. This was accompanied by dramatic reductions in alcohol-related problems, including a 33 per cent drop in cirrhosis deaths. Although there was some relaxation in restrictions after the War, there was understandably no return to the previous liberties. Consumption continued to fall and so did alcohol-related mortality.[1]

In recent years, alcohol campaigners have pointed to dramatic increases in consumption over the last three decades as the principal cause of increased drinking problems. We can see if this checks out by studying Table 4 which gives the appropriate figures for the fifteen years up until 1984.

International Comparisons

Some parties in the debate on alcohol misuse would contend that Britain has far less of a drink problem than other European countries. This view is well founded (see Figure 8) but should not give us cause for complacency. It is reckoned that France has a problem ten times the size of Britain's. We should therefore take care to learn from France's mistakes and ensure that we don't repeat them.

If we can determine some of the reasons for the differences between countries, we can be more certain of the best way to tackle Britain's problems. A study of European trends

TABLE 4

United Kingdom alcohol consumption per head of population and convictions for public drunkenness, drinking and driving convictions, cirrhosis mortality and hospital admissions for alcohol dependence, 1970–84

Year	UK alcohol consumption per head in litres of pure alcohol	UK drunkenness convictions per 10,000 pop.	Drinking and driving convictions in Britain per 10,000 pop.	Cirrhosis deaths in England and Wales per 100,000 pop.	English hospital first admissions for alcohol dependence per 100,000 pop.
1970	7.03	22.3	8.4	3.71	5.17
1971	7.37	23.4	11.7	4.19	5.70
1972	7.79	24.1	13.8	4.41	6.19
1973	8.61	26.6	16.0	4.77	7.34
1974	8.85	27.7	16.3	4.63	8.11
1975	8.82	27.9	16.6	4.82	8.40
1976	9.28	28.6	14.1	4.94	8.68
1977	8.81	28.2	12.7	4.73	9.17
1978	9.50	27.5	14.1	4.97	9.13
1979	9.79	29.9	15.6	5.60	9.74
1980	9.33	30.9	18.2	5.64	10.96
1981	8.89	27.1	16.5	5.59	10.55
1982	8.67	26.1	17.0	5.42	8.91
1983	8.83	25.7[1]	22.3[2]	5.47	8.63
1984	9.21	22.1[1]	22.8	5.67	9.46

1. These figures are for England and Wales only.
2. The 1981 Road Transport Act introduced evidential breath-testing machines in May 1983.

Note: All figures refer to the population aged fifteen or over.

Source: Royal College of Psychiatrists (1986), *Alcohol, Our Favourite Drug*, Tavistock.

over a thirty-year period provides some interesting pointers. While the post-war boom has led to an increase in alcohol consumption in every European country except France, which still tops the poll despite a 16 per cent fall in

FIGURE 8

Liver cirrhosis death rates and alcohol consumption in various countries in the mid-1970s.

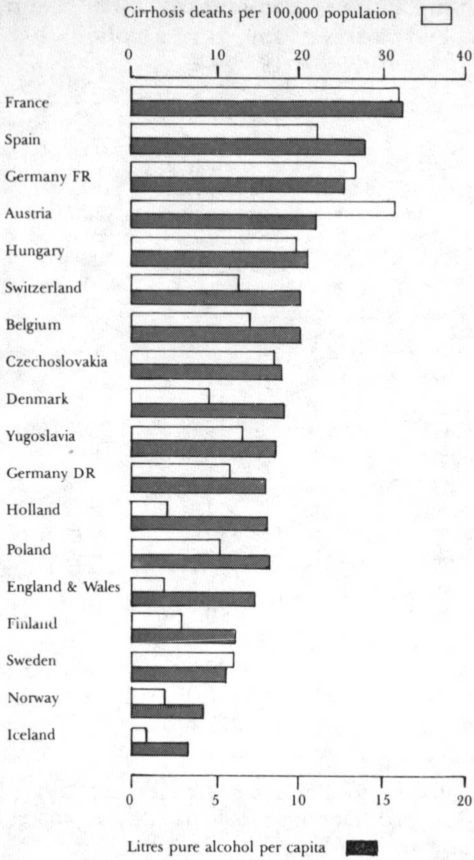

Source: Office of Health Economics (1981), *Alcohol—Reducing the Harm*, London.

consumption, those with the highest taxation and least pub opening hours have fared best.[2]

With this in mind, we should be concerned about the effects of the 1988 increases in the opening hours of England and Wales. Experts differ in their analysis of drinking trends in Scotland since similar changes took place there in 1976. The Scottish evidence indicates that there was no dramatic increase in consumption but there was a measurable reduction in drunkenness offences. However, some observers point out that the Scottish reforms coincided with the start of an economic recession and are reserving judgement until relevant mortality statistics (e.g. incidence of liver cirrhosis) are collated. The fear is that what might have been gained in reducing the consequences of *intoxication* will be lost through the long-term effects of increased *regular drinking*.

Influences on Consumption

As we have seen, there is overwhelming evidence to suggest that the level of consumption of alcohol in the nation is the major determinant of the extent of alcohol-related harm. If we are to see the problem reduced, we must see consumption fall. There are a number of influences on consumption which we should therefore consider.

(a) *Price and Disposable Income*

Changes in the price of alcohol could not alone account for the doubling of consumption in the U.K. between 1950 and 1979. Only when prices are related to disposable income can we see a clear relationship (see Figure 9). The message is clear. The more money we have in our pockets, the more we drink.

(b) *Availability*

The number of retail outlets for alcohol has been steadily increasing over the last thirty years. In 1976, the total number of on- and off-licensed premises in England and Wales was 116,167. In 1986, this figure had risen to 145,325, a 25 per cent increase. The increase in off-licences alone was over 33 per cent.[3]

Availability is affected by other factors. For example, women and young people are much more welcome in pubs than in the past. For women also, the off-licence section in supermarkets has increased the likelihood of them purchasing alcoholic drinks. The home-brew market has also taken off in a big way but there are no effective

FIGURE 9

Cost per pint of 100% alcohol as percentage of personal disposable income at current prices compared to annual consumption per head of population

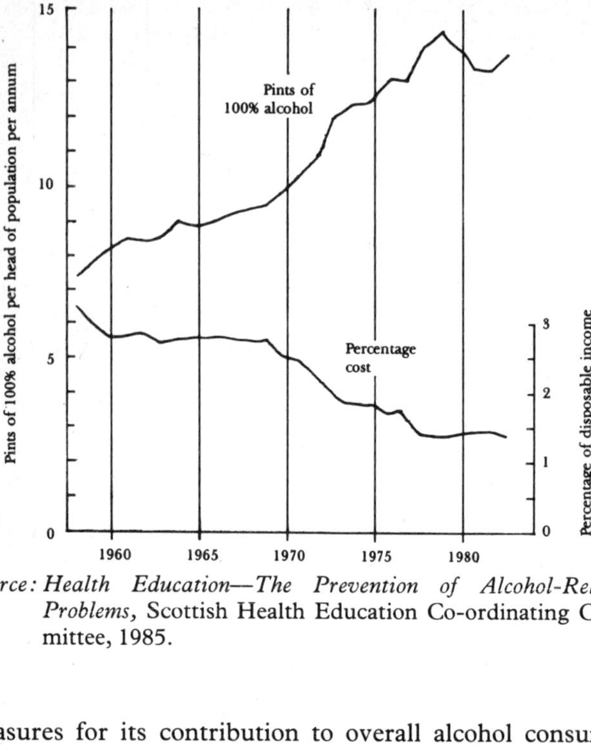

Source: Health Education—The Prevention of Alcohol-Related Problems, Scottish Health Education Co-ordinating Committee, 1985.

measures for its contribution to overall alcohol consumption.

Legislation restricts the availability of alcohol to particular groups. The under-fives should not be given alcohol. The under-eighteens should not purchase alcohol (except over-sixteens who can have beer and wine with a meal). Also, an intoxicated person should not be served alcohol. However, for legislation to be effective, it must be enforced and there is some evidence to suggest that many under-eighteens are finding it too easy to drink illegally. Ninety-three per cent of seventeen-year-old boys and 35 per cent of girls, in one survey, admitted to drinking illegally.[4] One consequence of the increase in the number of licensed premises is the difficulty in policing so many outlets.

(c) *Demand*

Alcohol producers spend £200 million per annum in an attempt to create demand for their brands.[5] While it is argued by the drinks industry that advertising is not a significant influence on overall consumption, it is evident that advertisers have been effectively encouraging two new markets for their products, namely women and young people. Women are now identified as the major purchasers of alcohol for household consumption and are targeted accordingly. New brands have been created to appeal specifically to women's tastes. Some advertising campaigns have been clearly aimed at the young. One cider producer openly acknowledged that they had single-mindedly set out to capture the eighteen to twenty-five age group and spent millions in the process.

(d) *Alternatives*

One of the most encouraging recent changes has been the introduction of 'low-alcohol' and 'alcohol-free' lagers and wines by the drinks industry. The impact of these products on the market has yet to be fully assessed but some of them have obviously become very popular. Established specialist distributors of these products (see Appendix C) have enjoyed a recent boom but even our biggest brewers are developing and marketing their own brands. The effect of this change has been to offer acceptable alternatives for all drinkers, and particularly those who want to drink less without looking out of place in a pub environment.

Accompanying this trend has been the establishment of several alcohol-free pubs around the country, some of them with a particular emphasis on attracting young people. Some organisations (see Appendix C) have taken a special interest in promoting developments of that kind and produce useful information for anyone interested. The main complaint about non-alcoholic drinks, particularly those purchased on licensed premises, is that they can be expensive, many costing more than their alcoholic equivalent.

In general terms, we have become a more health, fitness and diet-conscious society and many people appear to be adopting more active leisure interests than a 'night out at the local'. However, it is worth noting the number of sports and leisure centres which have a drinks licence, and those who sweat it out on the squash courts are sometimes expending as much energy in the bar afterwards.

As a footnote on alternatives, the churches might like to know that there are a number of substitutes for alcoholic communion wine on the market.

Group Pressures and Social Norms

Since so much social activity is culturally and group determined, the dynamics of group behaviour is an important dimension of alcohol use which should not be overlooked. To suggest that changes in price, in legislation, or in advertising standards could, by themselves, reduce problem drinking would be misleading.

Historical records suggest that over-reliance on legal and fiscal measures could, in the long term, be counter-productive. For example, Prohibition in the United States drove brewing and distilling into the control of racketeers. Public demand for alcohol sustained a substantial illegal industry throughout the Prohibition era and ultimately resulted in the repeal of the offending statute. More recently in Russia, rigid government restrictions, which had only been in force for a few years, have been relaxed in response to a boom in the illegal production of alcohol. Evidently, social dependency on alcohol can override government controls even to the extent of tolerating a black market in drinks.

In this country, there are significant regional variations in drinking behaviour which are unaccountable with respect to price and availability. For example, drinkers in the north of England tend to consume more than their southern counterparts. It is apparent that communities with a tradition of heavy engineering or mining tend to have the highest proportions of heavy drinkers. In these communities, the social norms for acceptable drinking levels have been passed on from generation to generation and will not be easily changed. Heavy or hard drinking is often associated with a 'macho' image and it is difficult for any individual to go against the tide. Even within less traditional social environments the practice of 'rounds' prevails. Consequently, in a group of eight drinkers, there is an inherent pressure on each to consume eight purchases from the bar. To 'pass' on one round is to risk losing value for money.

Yet there are many positive aspects of the social contexts in which people drink. Most licensed premises and clubs encourage a sense of community. Games, quizzes and pastimes accompany the consumption of alcohol. The village pub is often the hub of rural communities. It is warm, lively, welcoming and open seven days a week. In contrast, the parish church may be cold, draughty and open only one morning a week. However, there need be no conflict between the two and the parish priest may well be spending time in the pub, meeting with parishioners in a relaxed atmosphere and learning of needy situations.

Pubs often facilitate caring community responses to social needs. Many groups of 'regulars' pride themselves on their fund-raising exploits for local charities. On the individual level, an empty well-worn chair is noticed and someone will drop in at the home of its normal incumbent to see how he or she is faring. The quality of 'fellowship' in some pubs represents a challenge to the Church. We know that our faith equips us for the highest levels of human fellowship but is it always demonstrated as it should be?

Despite the most positive features of social drinking environments, they are notoriously weak in one respect. Their internal controls are apparently ineffective in the prevention of harmful drinking behaviour. The problem drinker generates acute discomfort in most drinking groups. In most cases, the problem drinker's peers do not know what to say or how to respond. Consequently, there is a great risk of social alienation and the problem drinker may lose the friends he once felt he could depend on.

In some structured drinking situations (e.g. licensed clubs) there is potential for establishing an 'Alcohol Policy' which all members can endorse. This could result in more effective group controls on drinking behaviour and in appropriate responses for individuals who get into difficulty. It is not apparent how similar controls could operate in a normal pub environment but perhaps the training of bar staff could include some guidance on how to identify problem drinkers and respond appropriately to them.

The challenge, therefore, is not only to make individuals think about their drinking but also to make groups 'think' about their social norms. It follows that some prevention initiatives should be targeted at particular groups. In our multi-cultural society, we must be sensitive to more than just regional and class variations. Ethnic differences are equally significant and demand careful attention. The task is a complex one and the Church, which unites Christians from a variety of backgrounds, has a unique role to play.

Many national agencies and institutions, including Alcohol Concern, Action on Alcohol Abuse and the Royal Medical Colleges have set out their agendas for action with particular reference to 'What the Government should do'. At the same time, all parties involved recognise that there are many levels and situations in which effective action can take place. We will consider the Church's contribution in the next chapter as we seek to put all the campaign issues into perspective.

7

THE WAY AHEAD

Seeking to establish a specific Christian approach to alcohol misuse in our society involves Church leaders with some major dilemmas. On the one hand, there is a need to make strong and clear statements concerning the dangers of alcohol misuse and, on the other, there is the challenge to help those who have a drinking problem.

It might be argued that the Church should disassociate itself from the cauldron of public debate and concentrate purely on caring for the individual problem drinkers and their families. However, the effectiveness of that care would, to a significant extent, be determined by the philosophy of the carer, and its acceptance by the one cared for. An express commitment to 'hate the sin and love the sinner', while in itself a legitimate Christian perspective, would not be readily received by one who had embraced the view that their drink problem was a 'sickness' rather than a 'sin'. It follows that the Church, while striving to be effective in practical caring, should be contributing to the ideological environment in which receptivity to Christian forms of help is moulded.

Absence from the public arena would also deny the Church's significant potential for involvement in prevention initiatives, especially if a rising generation is to be challenged to adopt radically different norms for drinking behaviour. While caring initiatives are directed at actual sufferers, prevention initiatives must be directed at potential sufferers —which means the whole population.

Present Trends

In the preceding chapters we have touched on some

historical perspectives concerning Christian responses to alcohol misuse. For example, nineteenth-century Christian action, in the form of the Temperance Movements, was a response to the growing prevalence of problem drinking in Victorian society. In this century there have been peaks and troughs in the consumption graphs and, presently, we seem to be on a high plateau.

While we might be relieved that the post-war rise in per capita consumption has finally peaked, there is certainly no room for complacency. The consequences of the last decade's heavy drinking may not be fully apparent until the under-25 portion of the population reach middle age and experience some belated symptoms of their youthful excesses. The Church's prophetic calling requires a long-term perspective on trends in our society.

In 1988, the Government relaxed licensing hours in England and Wales, allowing publicans to open their premises all day if they so wish. There were no immediate effects on the drinking population, no sudden increase in referrals to specialist agencies, but time will tell whether this change in legislation represented wisdom or folly.

At the same time as the Government is relaxing licensing hours, great concern is being expressed regarding some forms of drinking behaviour. The term 'lager louts' has been coined to describe groups of young people who frequently disturb the peace of rural villages as well as of city centres. In November 1988, Coventry became the first English city to adopt a 'no drinking in public places' byelaw. Other cities will follow in what is presently an experiment in reducing alcohol-related crime.

So, on the one hand, we witness relaxation in legislation and, on the other, new restrictions. Some may be confused by apparently mixed messages. The Church has a responsibility to give clear messages to every generation. It seems, however, that given growing public concern for young heavy drinkers in our society, we have a particular responsibility towards the next generation.

The Next Generation

In 1987, the Home Office Standing Conference on Crime Prevention published the 'Report of the Working Group on

Young People and Alcohol'. That group, chaired by Baroness Masham, had made a comprehensive survey of young persons' drinking behaviour with particular reference to its association with crime. Their report seemed to sum up the concern which was being felt by many agencies. Altogether, the picture was emerging of an alcohol problem in young people which dwarfed the 'big' problem of illicit drug use.

Some of the statistics related to problem drinking by the young are mentioned in Chapter 2. Alongside these, it is worth noting the proportion of young people in some of the general statistics. For example, the vast majority of convictions for drunkenness involve young men under twenty-one years of age.[1] Males under thirty dominate the figures for drivers killed in Britain who were over the legal blood-alcohol limit.[2]

While not all under-age drinkers are necessarily 'problem drinkers', they are certainly the most vulnerable group in the drinking population. This form of law breaking demonstrates the dominance of peer pressure over society's controls. Some youngsters, who use alcohol as a passport into the adult world, may end up using it as a crutch to cope with all sorts of adult pressures.

The problems of young people and alcohol are emerging against a backdrop of significant market changes. Liquor advertising and licensed facilities seem to be more and more appealing to the young. Some distributors have single-mindedly set out their stall to attract young men to a new product. The hidden message in so much drinks publicity is that 'to drink Brand X is to be strong and manly'. Some products are presented with great humour and the ads are not expected to be taken seriously or so they say. The reality is that the false messages are getting through and that too many young people see alcohol as a means to an end—as their ticket to masculinity or sophistication.

The young people who identify some difficulty with their drinking at an early stage are in the minority. Most are only pulled up short when their drinking and its effects begin to conflict with adult pressures and responsibilities. For some, it will be too late to redeem the waste.

Each year, a new set of young people is being faced with difficult choices concerning their use of alcohol. They are subject to many influences, not least their peers. If they are armed with basic facts about alcohol, if they have had an opportunity to think through the relevant issues and, if they have been exposed to good adult models of drinking behaviour, then there is a fair chance that they will not be taken in by the false messages and will make informed choices. These few 'IFs' represent a formidable challenge, especially to parents, teachers, and Church leaders as we consider our responsibilities to the next generation.

Campaigning for Change

It must be acknowledged that, with respect to campaigns against alcohol misuse, it is extraordinarily difficult to get the message right. In contrast, campaigns against smoking have a very simple message, 'Smoking is bad for you'. With respect to alcohol, there are some clear messages like 'Don't drink and drive'. This leaves people with a straight choice but, many 'sensible drinking' messages have tended to be ambiguous. In an attempt to overcome this difficulty, the term 'Drinkwise' has been used in a number of regional prevention programmes and represents an appeal to consumers to 'drink wisely'. Just as the national no-smoking day has proved its value, the proposed national 'Drinkwise' day (the first will take place in June 1989) should prove to be a useful innovation. Such major campaigns, which promote healthier drinking attitudes and behaviour, involve a substantial commitment of time and resources but they represent a tremendous leap forward in terms of public alcohol education.

While the positive publicity of the Health Education Authority's 'Drinkwise' campaigns is very welcome, most prevention issues at national level involve campaigners in persuading the government to adopt less popular measures (see Table 5).

Some national agencies do come together on occasions and present a united front. The Medical Royal Colleges, for example, issued a consensus statement in 1987, expressing their wish for an increase in alcohol prices. And, a 'Keep Alcohol Safeguards' campaign, against licensing law changes in 1988, involved a number of secular and Christian bodies. There is clearly a need for closer co-operation of all con-

TABLE 5

National Agenda for Action

Price increases (by taxation).
No relaxation of licensing hours.
Tighter controls on alcohol advertising.
Introduction of random breath-testing.
Increased penalties for drunken drivers.
Lowering of blood/alcohol driving limit.
Promotion of government-sponsored public education.
Promotion of professional training and research.
Increased government support for local services.
Alcohol education on the schools curriculum.

TABLE 6

Local Agenda for Action

The formation of local 'licensing forums' to monitor licensed premises and make appropriate representations to the police and magistrates.
The promotion of local health-promotion campaigns, e.g. Citywide 'Drinkwise' days.
The promotion of alcohol education in schools and youth clubs.
The promotion of alcohol awareness programmes for adult bodies, e.g. church groups.
The adoption of alcohol policies by companies, clubs, churches and other bodies.
The development of alcohol education schemes for young offenders.
The lobbying of local authorities requesting more resources for the development of alcohol services.
The promotion of alcohol-free bars and stalls at fêtes, sporting events, conferences, etc.
The development of 'get you home' transport schemes to discourage drunken drivers.

cerned and greater participation by church organisations.

Action on alcohol misuse at a local level reflects the national issues but involves more potential for achieving tangible goals in the short term.

Although some of the local proposals (Table 6)[3] may not find favour with all Christians, they nevertheless provide parish clergy and their congregations with an excellent opportunity to co-operate with other agencies in preventing alcohol problems in their locality.

The Role of the Church

The NCSA's Alcohol Awareness Programme provided an opportunity to collate the views of participating clergy on a number of relevant issues. The Church's role, with regard to problem drinking, was understood to have two main aspects:

- Its ability to offer psychological and practical support through Christian fellowship, church organisations and the clergy's own knowledge of, and contact with, the community: that is, the Church is seen as providing a 'structural base' for identifying and helping problem drinkers.
- Its ability to offer spiritual guidance, such that a problem with alcohol may be treated as a 'symptom' of a broader spiritual malaise which can be alleviated and finally overcome by prayer and Christian observance.

The above observations[4] are particularly relevant to the response of local churches and to the care of individual problem drinkers. The two aspects identified provide a useful framework for our consideration of the Church's contribution.

(a) *Support*

In this book, there have been a number of references to the complexity of the task in hand. However, it would be wrong to conclude that the problem of alcohol misuse should be left to 'the experts'. Whether specialist helping services are available or not, many problem drinkers will look to the Church for support. Clergy and lay pastoral workers are in the frontline of the community's response to alcohol misuse. The question is not, 'What will we do IF we encounter a problem drinker?', but 'What will we do WHEN we encounter a problem drinker?'

The same question applies to all Christians. Church members are also company directors, doctors, social workers, union shop stewards, civil servants, brewers and distillers. Christians function in every strata of society and in every trade and profession. To be both 'salt and light' in the world, Christians need to be responsive in all kinds of situations. Ill-equipped and unwary carers encounter many pitfalls in dealing with problem drinkers and, without the right perspective, the sincere efforts of concerned Christians may lead only to a sense of helplessness and frustration. Consequently, church leaders have a responsibility to ensure that the facts about alcohol and its effects are widely disseminated within the Church.

It must also be recognised that the clergy themselves are not immune from difficulties with their personal alcohol consumption and that some will require appropriate care and information. The NCSA Awareness Programme revealed that clergy were concerned that churches should have 'workplace policies' to ensure proper support for priests with a drinking problem.

As well as working alongside secular agencies, the Church can also promote the development of counselling services and residential establishments which provide a distinctive Christian programme for the care of problem drinkers. The Church of Scotland's Social Responsibility Committee have been at the forefront of this type of development North of the border, and their experiences may provide pointers for developments in the South. It follows that the more the Church is involved at the 'sharp end' of responses to alcohol misuse, the more credence will be given to its public statements and prevention initiatives.

(b) *Guidance*

Practical guidelines on alcohol consumption both for individual believers and for local churches, are required. While the Church should not be drawn into giving unequivocal approval for Christians to drink, those Christians

TABLE 7

The Church's Agenda for Action

The General Synod of the Church of England should consider the nature and extent of alcohol misuse in our society and develop a national strategy for responding to problem drinking in consultation with equivalent governing bodies in other denominations.

Members of the Church of England in both the House of Commons and the House of Lords, should seek to influence government policy on alcohol misuse by bringing Christian perspectives to bear on relevant debates.

The Church of England should adopt a 'Workplace Alcohol Policy' to ensure proper identification and care of any priests who experience alcohol-related problems.

The relevant Diocesan Boards and Councils should give priority to alcohol misuse and develop local strategies for prevention and caring initiatives.

Policies for alcohol use on church premises should be developed. With respect to social norms for drinking behaviour, Churches should adopt clear aims and objectives for themselves and for the communities they serve.

All forms of training and education in the Church should be reviewed to ensure that clergy and laity are properly equipped to teach about and respond to alcohol misuse.

Individual Christians should be encouraged to review their drinking practices and to adopt sensible guidelines.

---

who do drink should be aware of their personal and social responsibilities. The Government's agencies have not shrunk from recommending sensible drinking levels. A case can be made for the Church's endorsement of reasonable limits.

Any form of guidance should be prepared with great sensitivity to ensure that Christians, who do get into difficulty with their drinking, can approach their priest without fear of condemnation. Attention should also be given to workers in the drinks trade. Without clear direction, they might face some major dilemmas in reconciling their career with their Christian convictions.

Local churches are often involved in social events where alcohol may be present. Should the church fête offer bottles of wine as tombola prizes? Should alcohol be sold at church dances and socials? What action is appropriate if alcohol is brought into a youth club disco? Policies should be adopted which facilitate responsible decisions on these questions.

The NCSA's own alcohol awareness programme provides a useful model for further training and education initiatives in the Church. That programme is being extended to more dioceses as quickly as resources allow. There is a need for more investment in this and similar programmes. Moreover, wherever pastoral training is being planned and reviewed in the Church, there is a need to consider the introduction of an alcohol component, perhaps coupled with basic drugs and AIDS education, so that new generations of priests and deacons are fully equipped to respond to problems which will inevitably confront them.

While the provision of support and guidance may be the first two aspects of the Church's role with respect to alcohol misuse, a third challenge remains.

(c) *An Influence for Change*

To mobilise the Church and other social agencies requires a determined effort. This is not to suggest a revival of the nineteenth-century Temperance Movement. Certainly, the basic principles of temperance (not abstinence) may be reaffirmed, but the manifestations of alcohol misuse at the latter end of the twentieth century demand a multi-faceted response. The Church, through its local and national networks, is able to contribute to the process of change at every level of society and there are specific ways in which this can be achieved (Table 7).

Participants in the NCSA programmes identified a need for the Church to have a greater profile at national level with respect to alcohol misuse. Successive governments have consistently failed to adopt appropriate measures to combat alcohol misuse. The Church should not be silent on this issue and should seek ways to bring its influence to bear.

Traditional conceptions of alcohol misuse still appear to dominate the government's response. For example, there is an evident reluctance to taking strong action which would be 'unfair' on the vast majority of people. This is based on a view that only a 'small minority' of drinkers take risks with their drinking.

The NCSA, in its representations to the government,[5] have taken the following position:

> The NCSA does not consider that the extent of alcohol misuse in our society can be summed up by reference to the actions of a minority of the population. The social pressures, attitudes, values and customs which underpin all forms of alcohol use and misuse are nurtured, or at least tolerated, by the whole of society. Consequently, the NCSA favours prevention strategies which affect all alcohol consumers.

This notion that 'ALL' drinkers are at risk (just as all car drivers are at risk of accidents) is one that the government would do well to adopt. Such a change in posture could lead to radical changes in policy.

It is unlikely, however, that steps will be taken to reduce the alcohol consumption of the population until the government and electorate are convinced that the medical, economic, and social ill-effects of current consumption levels outweigh the pleasures and economic benefits. Nevertheless, some hope can be drawn from the establishment in 1987 of a Ministerial Group under the chairmanship of the Rt Hon. John Wakeham MP, to review policy on alcohol misuse.[6] In the Church of England, the House of Bishops and those who sit in the House of Lords have particular opportunities to present Christian perspectives on alcohol misuse.

Of course, if alcohol misuse is a matter for parliamentary concern, then it must also be given high priority by Diocesan Synods as well as the General Synod of the Church of England. Certainly, the Board for Social Responsibility's initiatives in preparing an information pack and publishing a policy statement (see Appendix B) are to be welcomed. However, if the Church is to engage seriously in tackling alcohol misuse, there must be a determination to take action at all levels and to encourage initiatives in all sectors of the Church. The issue is not simply finding new money. The Church's most precious resource is the time and commitment of its clergy and laity. Their contribution, as part of a co-ordinated approach with other agencies already committed to prevention, could have a significant impact in reducing the level of harm, caused through the misuse of alcohol in society.

NOTES

Introduction

1. Royal College of Psychiatrists (1986), *Alcohol, Our Favourite Drug.*
2. Royal College of Physicians (1987), *A Great and Growing Evil.* Royal College of General Practitioners (1986), *Alcohol, A Balanced View.*
3. World Health Organisation (1985), *Targets for Health for All.*
4. The research findings are summarised in *Alcohol and the Church* published by the NCSA, 1989.

Chapter 1

1. Royal College of Psychiatrists (1986), *Alcohol, Our Favourite Drug.*
2. Wilson, Paul (1980), *Drinking in England and Wales,* HMSO.
3. Action on Alcohol Abuse, London.

Chapter 2

1. Kendell, R. E. (1987), 'Drinking Sensibly', *British Journal of Addiction,* Volume 82.
2. Lockhart *et al* (1986), 'Detecting alcohol consumption as a cause of emergency general medical admissions', *Journal of Royal Society of Medicine,* Volume 79.
3. HMSO Annual Abstract of Statistics.
4. DHSS Mental Health Inquiry (1985), *Alcohol Abuse Hospital Statistics.*
5. Ritson, B. (1977), 'Alcoholism and Suicide' in *Alcoholism: New Knowledge and New Perspectives,* Croom Helm.
6. Transport and Road Research Laboratory.
7. Royal Lifesaving Society (1983), *Drownings in the British Isles.*
8. Department of Trade and Industry Report (1977).
9. *Ibid.*
10. Consumer Safety Unit: Department of Trade and Industry.
11. *Brewers' Society Statistical Handbook* (1984).
12. *Ibid.*
13. Hansard (13.1.86) col. 457—Written answer.

14. Gillies, N. (1976), 'Homicide in the West of Scotland', *British Journal of Psychiatry*, Volume 128.
15. Holtermann and Burchell (1981), *Government Economic Service Working Party*, No. 37, DHSS.
16. Harvard, J. (1972), 'Alcohol and Road Accidents' in *Alcoholism: New Knowledge and New Responses*, Croom Helm.
17. Department of Transport (1986), *Road Accidents in Great Britain.*
18. Royal Lifesaving Society (1983), *Drownings in the British Isles.*
19. Home Office (1985), *Statistical Bulletin*, Issue 33/85.
20. *Brewers' Society Statistical Handbook* (1986).
21. *Ibid.*
22. CSO (1987), *Annual Abstract of Statistics*, HMSO, and *Brewers' Society Statistical Handbook* (1986).
23. Creighton, S. J. (1984), *Trends in Child Abuse*, NSPCC.
24. Maynard, Hardman, & Whelan (1987), Data Note—9, *British Journal of Addiction*, Vol. 82.

Chapter 5

1. Kessell (1978), *Pattern and Range of Services*, DHSS Advisory Committee on Alcoholism.

Chapter 6

1. Royal College of Psychiatrists (1986), *Alcohol, Our Favourite Drug*, Tavistock.
2. P. Davies and D. Walsh (1983), *Alcohol Problems and Alcohol Control Policies in Europe*, Croom Helm.
3. Home Office (1986), *Statistical Bulletin*, Issue 37/86.
4. Davies, J. and Stacey, B. (1972), *Teenagers and Alcohol*, HMSO.
5. Action on Alcohol Abuse, London.

Chapter 7

1. Home Office (1985), *Statistical Bulletin*, Issue 33/85.
2. Masham (1987), *Young People and Alcohol*, Report of the Working Group on Young People and Alcohol, Home Office.
3. These proposals are drawn from the book: *Preventing Alcohol Problems—A guide to Local Action* by Tether, P. and Robinson D. (1986), Tavistock.
4. National Council for Social Aid (1989), *Alcohol and the Church.*
5. National Council for Social Aid (1988), *Memorandum to The Secretary of State for Health and Social Services.*
6. The NCSA's Memorandum to the Secretary of State for Health and Social Services (1988) contained a number of specific recommendations on preventing alcohol misuse.

Appendix A

TOPICS FOR DISCUSSION

The following points for discussion are intended to stimulate thinking on both the theological and the caring aspects of a Christian response to alcohol misuse. The aim is to cover most of the vital questions which are likely to arise as the Church seeks to tackle one of the most challenging features of the nation's social ills. Where appropriate, some Biblical references are given but the chosen passages are not expected to contain all the answers.

1. Pleasure or poison?

The Bible contains contrasting images of alcohol. Compare Psalm 104.15, Ecclesiastes 9.7, and John 2.1–11 with Isaiah 5.11–12 and Proverbs 23.29–35. On the one hand, the taste and the effects of wine are extolled. On the other, the consequences of too much wine are vividly described. Is there a sense in which partaking in some of the greatest pleasures in creation involves some of the greatest risks? Is it natural to want to know the limits of pleasure with respect to alcohol or is it sinful? We are exhorted to live by faith and not to give way to fear. Is there a way of enjoying alcohol in faith which will not result in harm. What might be the consequences of using alcohol without faith and/or in fear?

Our society places limits on most harmful substances. Some are banned, including natural plants. Is there a Christian principle which supports the use of alcohol and condemns the use of other drugs?

2. Individual or Corporate Responsibility?

A local brewery proposes to develop a new pub on the corner opposite your church. A number of church members protest about this and resolve to make individual objections to the relevant authorities. A youth leader is particularly incensed and suggests that the church organises a petition and that an objection be lodged on behalf of all the members. At first, it seems that this idea would be supported by all the members but it emerges that a significant minority are in favour of having a pub in what has previously been a 'dry' area. A few members actually work for the brewery concerned and feel that the protests are unfairly affecting their livelihood. It is argued that the church would be seen as being 'killjoy' and that any protest should be a matter of personal conviction. In response, it is argued that the church cannot remain silent about a development on its doorstep which could encourage local young people into a drinking environment and lead to trouble on the streets. Those who support the protest believe that the church should act corporately in line with the convictions of a majority of its members. How might this matter be resolved? What teaching would be appropriate in this situation?

3. 'Love bears all things'

A church member is married to a man with a serious drink problem. He has been physically violent towards her and verbally aggressive to the three young children. The situation has been worsening over recent years and there are serious financial problems. The children's behaviour is causing concern to teachers and social services have been involved. Friends have counselled the wife to take action but she stubbornly refuses. She states that she must be faithful to her husband and believes that her love for him will win in the end. She tends to cover up for him but is obviously getting more and more worried about the children. The risk is that, if she refuses to put her husband out or leave him, one incident could lead to them all being taken into care. How can this woman come to the point of taking firm action when she feels that the withdrawal of her love will spell downfall for her husband. Love is described one way in 1 Corinthians 13 and another in Hebrews 12. 5–11. Can she learn to express love in a firm way, setting clear limits for her husband's behaviour?

4. Victim or abuser?

A young single mum is involved in a church's young mothers' toddler group. It becomes apparent that she has a drinking problem which leads to occasional neglect of her child. The women who befriend her learn that she was abused as a child and as a teenager in her first relationships with men. She copes with her deep hurts and her relationship difficulties by drinking. Alcohol bridges the gap between her fear of men and her yearning for love and acceptance. The combination of alcohol and her emotional traumas influences her perception of the child's needs and she often responds inappropriately. It is feared that she will not be able to cope with the growing emotional demands of her child and that some sort of breakdown is inevitable. Those who are not so close to her see her as wanton and careless and a potential child abuser. Those who are closest are trying desperately to help someone who is becoming increasingly alienated.

When did this young woman cease to be a victim and became an abuser? Have Christians anything to offer her which professional services cannot provide? Are there any pointers for us in Jesus' responses to the two women in John 4.5–29 and John 7.53 to 8.11?

5. Sin or Sickness?

There is a continuing philosophical debate concerning the origins of addiction to alcohol and drugs. There are those who claim that habitual drunkenness is a form of learned behaviour, i.e. the result of a series of wrong choices. Opposing this view is the concept of 'alcoholism' or 'chemical dependency' as a sickness which is genetically determined. Is there a Christian perspective which can reconcile this polarisation? Is the concept of universal sin (Romans 3.23) compatible with either or both of these opposite views? Is Paul's personal struggle with sin, recorded in Romans 7.15–25, comparable with the problem drinker's experience of fighting alcohol dependency? In terms of personal responsibility, what are the implications of identifying a problem as a sickness compared with confessing it as a sin? Is the message of 1 John 5–10 relevant to this discussion?

Appendix B

SUGGESTIONS FOR FURTHER READING

1. General Literature

The following books provide useful information on many aspects of problem drinking. This section includes books which examine the social and environmental factors which determine patterns of drinking behaviour.

Alcohol Concern (1987), *The Drinking Revolution.*

Board for Social Responsibility (1988), *Alcohol Misuse—A Statement*, The General Synod of the Church of England.

Board for Social Responsibility (1987), *Information Pack on Alcohol*, The General Synod of the Church of England.

Cavanagh, J. and Clairmonte, F. F. (1985), *Alcoholic Beverages: Dimensions of Corporate Power*, Croom Helm, London.

Davies, P. and Walsh, D. (1983), *Alcohol Problems and Alcohol Control in Europe*, Croom Helm, London.

Dorn, N. (1983), *Alcohol, Youth and the State*, Croom Helm, London.

Edwards, G. and Grant, M. (1980), *Alcoholism Treatment in Transition*, Croom Helm, London.

Glatt, M. M. and Marks, J. (eds) (1982), *The Dependence Phenomenon*, MTP Press.

Golding, P. (ed.) (1980), *Alcoholism, a Modern Perspective*, MTP Press.

Grant, M. and Ritson, B. (1983), *Alcohol, the Prevention Debate*, Croom Helm, London.

Heather, N. and Robertson, I. (1986), *Problem Drinking*, Pelican Books.

Heather, N., Robertson, I., and Davies, P. (eds) (1985), *The Misuse of Alcohol (Crucial issues in Dependence Treatment and Prevention)*, Croom Helm, London.
Hore, B. D. and Grant, M. (1981), *Alcohol Problems in Employment*, Croom Helm, London.
Jesper, A. (1986), *Non-alcoholic Cocktails*, Whittet Books with Leisure Drinks.
McConville, B. (1983), *Women Under the Influence*, Virago Press.
Masham, Baroness (Chairman) (1987), *Young People and Alcohol—Report of the Working Group on Young People and Alcohol*, Home Office.
Orford, J. (1985), *Excessive Appetites*, Wiley, Chichester.
Parry Lewis, J. (1985), *Freedom to Drink*, The Institute of Economic Affairs, London.
Royal College of Psychiatrists (1986), *Alcohol: Our Favourite Drug*, Tavistock, London.
Scott, C. (1988), *Alcohol-free Bars*, Alcohol Concern.
Tether, P. and Robinson, D. (1986), *Preventing Alcohol Problems—A Guide to Local Action*, Tavistock, London.

2. Helping the Problem Drinker

This section refers to books which will be of particular value to Christians engaged in helping problem drinkers. Some general books on counselling are included, although not all are written from a Christian viewpoint.

Alcohol Concern (1988), *Teaching about Alcohol Problems (A Training Manual)*, Woodhead Faulkner, London.
Campbell, A., *Rediscovering Pastoral Care*, Darton, Longman and Todd.
Collins, G., *Christian Counselling*, Word Books.
Davies, I. and Raistrick, D. (1981), *Dealing with Drink—A handbook for helping problem drinkers*, BBC Publications.
Dobson, J. C., *Love Must Be Tough*, Hodder and Stoughton.
Dunn, J., *God is for the Alcoholic*, Moody Press.
Grant, M. (1984), *Same Again: A Guide to Safer Drinking*, Penguin.

Heather, N. and Robertson, I. (1986), *Problem Drinking*, Pelican Books.

Huggett, J. (1988), *Listening To Others*, Hodder and Stoughton.

Kennedy, E., *On Becoming a Counsellor*, Gill and Macmillan.

Robertson, I. and Heather, N. (1986), *Let's Drink to Your Health!: A self-help guide to sensible drinking*, British Psychological Society, Leicester.

Simnett, I., Wright, L. and Evans, M. (1984), *Drinking Choices* (*Alcohol Education Manual*), Health Education Council/TACADE.

Stockwell, T. and Clement, S. (eds) (1987), *Helping the Problem Drinker*, Croom Helm, London.

Wholey, Dennis *et al* (1986), *The Courage to Change*, Fontana/Collins.

Appendix C

LIST OF USEFUL ADDRESSES

For information on training and education resources, including audio-visual material and current statistics:

Alcohol Concern, 305 Gray's Inn Road, London WC1X 8QF
Telephone 01-833 3471

Action on Alcohol Abuse, 11 Carteret Street, London SW1H 9DL
Telephone 01-222 3454

Health Education Authority, Hamilton House, Mabledon Place, London WC1H 9TX
Telephone 01-631 0930

Medical Council on Alcoholism, 1 St Andrew's Place, London NW1 4LB
Telephone 01-487 4445

Campaign Against Drinking and Driving—CADD, Livingstone House, 11 Carteret Street, London SW1H 9DL
Telephone 01-222 3454

TACADE (Teachers' Advisory Council on Alcohol and Drug Education), Head Office, 2 Mount Street, Manchester M2 5NG
Telephone 061-834 7210

Churches Council on Alcohol and Drugs, 4 Southampton Row, London WC1B 4AA
Telephone 01-242 6511

Institute of Alcohol Studies, Alliance House, 12 Caxton Street, London SW1H 0QS
Telephone 01-222 4001; 01-222 5880

Brewers' Society, 42 Portman Square, London W1H 0BB
Telephone 01-486 4831

'Stay Dry' Campaign, Alliance House, Caxton Street, London SW1M 0QS
Telephone 01-222 5880

The Band of Hope, Hope House, 48 Great Peter Street, London SW1P 3LT
Telephone 01-222 6809

Institute for the Study of Drug Dependence, 1–4 Hatton Place, Hatton Garden, London EC1 8ND
Telephone 01-430 1991

Leisure Drinks Ltd., 24 Willow Road, Trent Lane, Castle Donnington, Derby
Telephone 0332 850616

For information on local advisory services and self-help groups:

Alcohol Concern, 305 Gray's Inn Road, London WC1X 8QF
Telephone 01-833 3471

Alcoholics Anonymous, General Service Office, P.O. Box 1, Stonebow, York YO1 2NJ
Telephone 0904 644026

Al-Anon Family Groups, 61 Great Dover Street, London SE1 4Y. (Al-Ateen can also be contacted here)
Telephone 01-403 0888

Drinkwatchers, 200 Seagrave Road, London SW6 1RQ
Telephone 01-727 9447; 01-381 3155

Drugs, Alcohol, Women, Nationally—DAWN, Boundary House, 91–93 Charterhouse Street, London EC1M 6HR
Telephone 01-250 3284

Turning Point, CAP House, 9–12 Long Lane, London EC1A 9HA
Telephone 01-606 3947

Accept Services, 200 Seagrave Road, London SW6 1RQ
Telephone 01-381 3155

The Aquarius Centres, The White House, 111 New Street, Birmingham B5 7SL
Telephone 021-632 4727

Medical Council on Alcoholism, 1 St Andrew's Place, London NW1 4LB
Telephone 01-487 4445